Praise for *A Clearing Season*

In *A Clearing Season,* Sarah Parsons masterfully illustrates a way to invite God into our quiet space so that we can fully experience the Lenten season. By giving ourselves permission to "make a way in the wilderness and rivers in the desert" (Isa. 43:19), we become freer and more willing to explore areas where we may not be satisfied. The weekly readings in this book gently nudge us to live through the temptations and "wild beasts" we experience during the forty days of Lent—a clearing season. If you want to release the need to control your surroundings, see yourself as you truly are, or learn to accept the gift of quietness that the Lenten season may bring, *A Clearing Season* is a must read.

—TRENAY PERRY BYNUM
Author of *Triumph! The Beautiful Face of Courage*
Founder and director, Figures of Nashville, Inc.

Sarah Parsons' thoughtful book acknowledges the biblical tradition of soul searching. Exercises and questions probe and direct the reader toward the ultimate goal of the Lenten season: to draw closer to God. Her step-by-step process moves the reader from the wilderness—a place of life's chaos—to the establishment of new, enriching patterns. The detailed guide for small groups includes excellent preparation and exercises. *A Clearing Season* is a well-grounded, hopeful work that will be useful year after year to individuals and groups as they partake of Easter's promise of new life.

—BONNIE EPPERLY-TRUDEL, EdD
Licensed Professional Counselor
Mental Health Service Provider
Naples, Florida

Every year I approach Lent with the same feeling—dread. I know I'm going to attempt to avoid something I enjoy for reasons I'm not completely sure of and fail to make it through forty days. But after reading *A Clearing Season,* the season of Lent seems more doable and more meaningful. It makes Lenten more personal and more honest to the "everyday" seeker. Who knew it was okay to start small and to suffer setbacks? Sarah Parsons' writing guides and encourages us to truly find God in life's chaos and to use Lent as a time to clear a path to a deeper faith. Simply put, this book is good!

—BRANDON DYCE
Graduate student
DePaul University

I was immediately captured by Sarah Parsons' honest approach to my favorite season of the year. Filled with relevant stories and creative Lenten practices, *A Clearing Season* provides an incredible guide for individuals or small groups to use in preparation for Easter. This book is an essential addition to the library of anyone on the journey who is ready to clear space for God during the season of Lent.

—CIONA ROUSE
Freelance writer and youth/young adult specialist
Nashville, Tennessee

a clearing season

REFLECTIONS FOR LENT

SARAH PARSONS

UPPER
ROOM BOOKS®
NASHVILLE

No part of this book may be reproduced in any manner whatsoever without permission except for brief quotations in critical articles or reviews. For information, write Upper Room Books, 1908 Grand Avenue, Nashville, TN 37212.

The Upper Room® Web site: www.upperroom.org

Upper Room®, Upper Room Books®, and design logos are trademarks owned by The Upper Room®, Nashville, Tennessee. All rights reserved.

Scripture quotations are from the New Revised Standard Version Bible, copyright © 1989 by the Division of Christian Education of the National Council of the Churches of Christ in the United States of America. Used by permission. All rights reserved.

At the time of publication all Web sites referenced in this book were valid. However, due to the fluid nature of the Internet, some addresses may have changed or the content may no longer be relevant.

Cover and interior design: Nancy Terzian / Nterdesign
Cover photo: Foggy Woodlands © Royalty-Free / CORBIS
Fourth printing: 2007

Library of Congress Cataloging-in-Publication Data
Parsons, Sarah, 1971–
  A clearing season : reflections for Lent / by Sarah Parsons.
      p. cm.
  ISBN-13: 978-0-8358-9817-1
  ISBN-10: 0-8358-9817-2
  1. Lent—Meditations. I. Title.
  BV85.P323 2005
  242'.34—dc22
                                              2005006068

Printed in the United States of America

For my parents,
whose weekly presence on the second row at St. George's
first taught me to love spiritual disciplines

acknowledgments

Thank you, first of all, to JoAnn Miller and Upper Room Books for giving me the chance to write this book. The opportunity alone has been a tremendous gift. I am also grateful to Kathleen Stephens, who remembered that I like Lent and suggested me as a writer. Beth Richardson first helped me discover my interest in Lent by giving me a chance to edit seasonal reflections, and John Mogabgab has guided me through many turns on my career path. I am grateful to you and all my friends at The Upper Room who have given me so many blessed first chances.

My friends kept my spirits up and talked me through many a freak-out while I was writing this book. Thank you to Carrie Mills, Beth Lamb, Krissie McReynolds, Claire Turchi, Carrie Plummer, Dan Kearns, Dave Bone, Lissa Merritt, Isaac Deter-Wolf, Dana Hardy, Hugh Seid, and to my siblings—Annie Lattanzi, Catherine Parsons, and Will Parsons.

Finally, I dedicate this book to my parents, Lynn and Bill Parsons. How do I begin? They have made all my work possible through their unfailing love, support, and encouragement. If I can give the world half as much as they have given me, I will feel like a success.

contents

Acknowledgments   6

Introduction   8

Week 1 / Exploring the Wilderness   13

Week 2 / First Clearing   27

Week 3 / Natural Rhythms   41

Week 4 / New Growth   55

Week 5 / Weathering Storms   67

Week 6 / Consecration   79

Epilogue / Easter Sunday   91

Group Exercises   93

Appendix / Suggested Lenten Practices   107

Notes   109

About the Author   111

introduction

People think it's strange to like Lent. It is, after all, a penitential season, and who enjoys penitence? The very word *penitence* brings to mind images of monks sitting in dark rooms wearing hair shirts. Feeling penitent sounds bad enough, but actually *liking* Lent seems to verge on masochism. It sounds as if one enjoys scrutinizing the past, dragging out every misdeed, and wallowing in guilt for six weeks.

However, Lent is not all about penitence or misdeeds or guilt. It is a time of introspection, true, but its ultimate purpose lies beyond penitence. In essence Lent serves as our annual invitation to come closer to God. It provides a time to look at our lives and ourselves, not so we may criticize ourselves more harshly but so we can identify the obstructions that keep us from God. What keeps us from feeling the presence of the divine in our every day? How do we hide from God, and why? Lent gives us a chance to look at such obstructions and to move them gently away so that we can come closer to the Love that gives us life, the Love whose triumph we will celebrate on Easter morning.

Thus Lent offers a gift of time and a promise of closeness. It gives us time to see our current state of affairs in complete honesty. Furthermore, it gives us time to compare this present snapshot with an image of where we would like to be, a place we feel God wants us to find. Self-scrutiny is part of Lent's process, but we do not observe Lent for the sake of self-scrutiny alone. To sit too long with the guilt and shame of our misdeeds would, in fact, go against the gospel message. Christ's message is one of new life and forgiveness, so Lenten self-scrutiny must serve this purpose.

To arrive at newness of life, we first name the parts of our lives that are shrouded in darkness, the parts of ourselves where life does not flourish. We walk through some muck so that we can leave it behind us and find Easter joy beyond. Following close upon Lent's penitence is hope—hope that the barriers between us and God will not remain, that with God's help we will clear them away and begin to experience greater joy and newness of life.

If we picture all the obstructions between us and God as a wilderness, Lent presents us with time to clear and cultivate a part of that wilderness, to create an open space in it. In this newly opened space, we may live more freely and commune more closely with the divine. We can transform this wilderness and make it our home, our garden, a place that invites God in and asks God to stay. Our wilderness needs to be ordered differently so we can move more freely in it, so we can, as God does in Isaiah, "make a way in the wilderness and rivers in the desert" (Isa. 43:19).

How to Use This Book

This book progresses through Lent with one chapter for each week. Week 1, "Exploring the Wilderness," extends for a week and a half, beginning with Ash Wednesday and concluding on the second Sunday in Lent. Each of the following weeks is designed to begin on Monday and end on Sunday, in time for a group meeting about that chapter on Sunday.

You may read the entire week's chapter at the beginning of the week, or you may read one chapter section each day. Read

> If we picture all the obstructions between us and God as a wilderness, Lent presents us with time to clear and cultivate a part of that wilderness, to create an open space in it.

at least the first section of each chapter at the beginning of the week, because it offers an individual exercise to engage in throughout the week.

The chapters move through a process of clearing space, beginning in the chaotic wilderness and ending in an open space, which awaits the in-breaking of new life on Easter morning.

Week 1: In the first week, we let ourselves enter the wilderness parts of our lives. In other words, we begin to look at the aspects of our lives and ourselves that feel chaotic or out of control. This wilderness includes any thoughts, actions, or feelings that hinder our communication with God or our sense of God's presence. This first week provides time simply to name obstructions and chaos—to look around us, as scary and painful as that may be, and see what interferes with our relationship with God.

Week 2: In the second week of Lent, we will begin a Lenten practice that grows out of our first week's observations. Considering any obstructions found during the first week, you will choose one to clear away with a relevant Lenten practice. One obstacle to a felt connection with God is lack of time spent with God. Many of us have responsibilities that keep us busy during all our waking hours; we move quickly from one task to the next, feeling that we have no time for prayer. If you identify busyness as a major obstacle to your relationship with God, a good Lenten practice might be to clear ten minutes per day for prayer. By initiating such a practice, you begin to open yourself to God.

Week 3: During the third week of Lent, we will focus on our chosen practice and look for patterns developing in it. If we are to devote ourselves to the process of clearing space, finding a practice that suits us personally is important. This will be the week to watch for your own best spiritual practices: What truly brings you closer to God? If a Lenten practice resembles the work of clearing room for a garden, this week is the one that invites us to identify when and how we do our own best work.

Week 4: The fourth week of Lent offers time to stop and observe the new growth appearing in our lives as a result of clearing space. During this week, we will notice progress and express gratitude for any new growth we discover. We will watch for ways in which we have come closer to God, ways in which we may have become more loving, more creative, more open to God's unexpected action in the world. We will celebrate this evidence of new growth and look for ways to nurture it further, so that it can come into full flower.

Week 5: The fifth week of Lent focuses on handling setbacks to practice. Any new discipline falters at some point. This week provides time to consider honestly the times we have faltered and to look for blessings hidden in each slip. Setbacks may benefit our practice in the long run by increasing our commitment and by making us aware of our need for others and of our ultimate dependence on God.

Week 6: As Lent moves toward its close and we enjoy any openness that our Lenten practice has created, Holy Week invites God's consecration. Holy Week encourages us to experience our cleared space as holy ground and to attend more closely to the holy in our lives. It is also a time of keeping vigil and waiting for God's light to illuminate and nurture the space we have opened and prepared.

Whatever shape this season takes for you, may Lent open you to greater freedom, life, and love. May your work clear space for you to enjoy God and rest in God's presence, and may you find the living Christ resurrected in you on Easter morning.

WEEK 1

exploring the wilderness

The Spirit immediately drove [Jesus] out into the wilderness. He was in the wilderness forty days, tempted by Satan; and he was with the wild beasts; and the angels waited on him.

—Mark 1:12-13

Lent begins in the wilderness. Jesus is driven there, implicitly against his will, by the Spirit who knows that he needs to go. He stays in the wilderness forty days, and there he encounters Satan, the very worst that human imagination can conjure. Jesus sits with wild beasts, and he is cared for by divine beings who presumably make his stay bearable.

This is the first Gospel story the Sunday Lenten lectionary would have us contemplate. From it we learn several things. First, we learn where we should begin. We discover that even against our better judgment, we must begin these forty days by going alone to a wild place—in ourselves or in our lives. If we are fiercely honest with ourselves as we begin a Lenten journey toward greater openness, we must start by seeing things we would rather not see.

This passage also teaches us what we will find in the wilderness. If our experience resembles that of Jesus, then the

INDIVIDUAL EXERCISE

Each day during this week, spend time in quiet solitude, thinking about wilderness. If you don't already have a regular prayer time, begin with ten to fifteen minutes a day. When you sit in your chosen solitary place, distractions likely will bombard you. This is normal.

Breathe deeply and relax. Identify the thoughts that enter your consciousness. Especially notice your fears and worries or anything that feels overwhelming or chaotic; these are the denizens of your own hallowed wilderness. You may experience a feeling of being overworked, of having no time for rest. You may become aware of anxiety about relationships, a feeling that your interactions with others are somehow out of balance. You may feel an emptiness, a sense that you want to do something—perhaps some activity or task you have avoided. An element of wilderness exists in all these situations; these are the parts of ourselves we tend to fight against. These are also the parts of ourselves that we will begin to befriend, settling them down and clearing more internal space.

Don't worry about clearing space in this wilderness just yet; plenty of time remains for that later in the season. Observe any tendency to judge yourself harshly about the nature of your wilderness. For now just note a few places where you feel out of control, overwhelmed, or blocked and list them in a journal that only you will see. In this way, you map your own inner wilderness, and you can later decide how to focus your Lenten work. For now just observe and take notes.

passage tells us that wilderness is an important and valuable place, not to be overlooked. We tend, especially in Western society, to separate ourselves from discomfort or chaos. This passage counsels us to try a different approach. It encourages us to sit in the uncomfortable, chaotic place, possibly for a long time. Rather than running from the wilderness, Jesus stays there as long as necessary, long enough to experience it fully.

The passage also lets us know that we will be tempted in this wilderness, perhaps powerfully. We will encounter forces internal and external that seem wild to us, like beasts, unfamiliar and unpredictable. At the same time, we will be cared for, even in this wild place, with angelic strength and tenderness.

Beginning with Ash Wednesday, we are asked—or perhaps driven—to enter the wilderness. Finding wilderness places is not difficult when we have the courage to look. The best way to find them is to set aside some time free of distractions, as little as fifteen minutes, and sit in a quiet place for that time. The very act of sitting alone quietly can bring the wilderness to the fore; at such times, fears, worries, and anxieties accost us. As troubling as the prospect may be, this barrage of fears, worries, and anxieties is exactly what we seek during this first week of Lent. We are driven to this wilderness, asked to sit in it, get to know it, and ultimately befriend its inhabitants.

DRIVEN OUT

According to the Synoptic Gospel accounts, Jesus is driven into the wilderness after he receives God's blessing and before he begins his work in the world. The wording—"the Spirit . . . drove him"—leads us to believe that Jesus did not choose to go to the wilderness on his own. The Spirit gave him a push, and he acquiesced. At the beginning of Lent, we also may find ourselves a little hesitant, even unwilling. Jesus' story alerts us to a helpful bit of information at the outset of a wilderness venture: We don't have to *want* to enter the wilderness; we just have to go.

I remember a wilderness time in my own life, a time that seemed very dark, in which I felt lost, and to which I certainly was driven. When I went away to college, I left behind a world in which I had felt like a star. I had been a straight-A student. I had acted in plays, sung in musicals, and been elected student body president in my junior year. I had won the history award, run cross-country, and done service projects. I thought I could do it all and excel at it all, and surely this would never change. I would be a star all my life, revered by my peers, whom I would treat with benevolence and magnanimity.

Lo and behold, when I got to Yale, I found a sea of people much like me. Some of them were, to my horror, bigger stars than I. My first impulse, of course, was to trounce them all. I would simply have to climb to the top of the heap the way I had in high school. I set to work, anticipating my easy victory and eventual rise to fame, which might include an illustrious career in law and appointment to the Supreme Court, surely culminating in my landslide election to the presidency.

Unfortunately, getting to the top of the Yale heap required a lot of work. The competitive freshman humanities program I entered demanded a paper a week and hundreds of pages of reading. Every extracurricular activity—even in community service organizations—required first an application and interview, and then, once selected, a major time commitment. Sports were out of the question, as I had trailed the pack in high school. Still, I tried to do it all, and on a good night I got six hours of sleep. I was barely keeping up, not even close to standing out. I felt exhausted, terrified, and utterly alone; but I didn't know how to stop pushing myself.

I didn't choose to enter a wilderness of depression, but I was led to one that year. Although I did not see it at the time, I needed that wilderness year to move from one identity—the confining identity of superstar high school student—to another, fuller identity, one truer to my real self. To get there,

I had to go through a period of great loss and confusion. As I got more honest with myself about who I was and what I wanted, I had to let go of many old self-identifiers. Although the process was painful and frightening, I was freer to be myself when I emerged.

Many people, at some point in their lives, have experiences like my first year of college. People recovering from addictions talk about the necessity of "hitting bottom" before they begin to make changes. The bottom is a dark, scary place, a place that people unwillingly hit only when all their best evasion tactics have stopped working.

The story of Jonah in the fish's belly tells of being driven to wilderness, and it reminds us of God's hand in the business:

> You cast me into the deep,
>   into the heart of the seas,
> and the flood surrounded me. . . .
> The waters closed in over me;
>   the deep surrounded me;
> weeds were wrapped around my head
>   at the roots of the mountains.
> I went down to the land
>   whose bars closed upon me forever. (Jonah 2:3, 5-6)

Jonah, profoundly lost, feels close to death and states clearly that God sent him there. If God chooses to send us to such terrifying places, then we must sometimes need them. God does not, of course, leave any of us there alone, but the Spirit knows when we need to go.

Western culture tends to resist emotional pain and unhappiness. Our world, full of smiling faces in television ads, celebrates wealth and recreation as "the good life." In many ways, it is a world of Prozac and quick fixes. There is nothing wrong with smiling or recreation or Prozac; happiness, vacations, and solutions are wonderful gifts when we get them. But we are also human, and to be human means living a life of ups and downs, experiencing the full range of emotions from great joy to great sorrow. To resist sorrow, pain, anxiety, and confusion is tantamount to refusing to be human, and we lose much rich experience and closeness to God when we refuse to be our full selves.

At the beginning of Lent, driven into the wilderness, we may hear our happiness-loving culture whisper in our ears, "You're taking the wrong path." We may think we're making a mistake, because according to TV commercials and conventional wisdom, feelings of elation always accompany the right path. However, when we are faithful and honest, the right path sometimes leads "through the narrow door" (Luke 13:24). Only we, with God's help, can decide which path we are meant to take.

When we look out toward this wilderness, it's okay if we feel totally unwilling to go and the Spirit has to drive us there kicking and screaming. Still the wilderness will serve its purpose: it will cleanse, teach, try, and still us. Entering the wilderness means leaving the comfortable to experience the uncomfortable for a time; it means choosing the sometimes difficult learning experience. And we all occasionally need a little Spirit-driving to get us out there.

Allowing oneself to be driven into the wilderness may be the greatest accomplishment of a Lenten experience. Even if this were your only Lenten experience, it would bring you to a deeper self-understanding, and your risk would bring you rewards. Just listening to the Spirit's guidance and choosing fearlessly to go where it leads—heedless of a world urging you to come back—brings a closeness to God and can be a great teacher.

The beauty of being driven into the wilderness is that you do not have to find your way there. Neither do you have to pretend that you want to go. All you have to do is open yourself to the possibility that some chaos, some wild energy, lives within you, and God will show you how to find it. You can go into it fussing every step of the way. God will show you parts of yourself that you may not wish to see, but God also will comfort you and show you truth; and from truth you can expect new humility, energy, and freedom.

FORTY DAYS

Lent is a long season, especially when you sit and think. In some traditions the season seems almost punitive, a long period of self-flagellation and self-denial. If you've ever seen the movie *Chocolat*, you know what this version of Lent looks like: a long season in a gray town with townspeople monitoring one another's observance, raising the alarm if they see someone dancing, laughing, eating chocolate, or otherwise enjoying life.

The Lenten season indeed lasts a long time, but its purpose is not, as the above stereotype would have us believe, for imposing on us a prolonged experience of pain. Rather, this long time is a gift. Originating in the fourth century, Lent was targeted toward the catechumenate, the group of persons preparing to join the church. The length of the season gave them time to consider their decision and prepare themselves for committed involvement in a new community. In a way, the Lenten season was long in order to give them the freedom to choose, to reconsider, to back out if they wanted. Now Lent offers us the same gift—a long time to examine where we have been and where we want to go in our spiritual lives. We don't have to make any snap decisions. We are free to think about options in the privacy of our own relationships to God, and to choose how we'll move forward. Lent affords a little time to calm down, breathe deeply, and then make some considered choices.

Lent also offers the gift of in-between time. As frightening as it may be at first, this long wilderness stay lets us sit between one place and the next. If "forty days" is biblical language for "a long time," then it appears we have as much time as we need here, in between. In this way, Lent reminds me of time spent in travel: when I am in an airport or actually in an airplane, my

> Lent offers the gift
> of in-between time.

mind is free to roam. Neither at home nor yet at my destination, I have no daily rituals or familiar conversation partners to direct my thinking. I think whatever I want. Travel time is much the same as Lenten wilderness time; you are neither here nor there, so your spirit is not bound up in its usual structures. It moves about freely, and if you take some time to write down your thoughts, you may be surprised at what emerges.

Lent lasts forty days, a long time, because we need a good stretch of time to step back and be neither here nor there. We need plenty of time to drop our old ways of doing things and live in-between, not yet knowing what the new ways of doing things will be. Living in-between can be scary. But taking the full forty days is important; not to do so would be like denying ourselves a spiritual adventure, the gift of in-between time.

TEMPTATIONS

I used to have recurring dreams about climbing staircases, narrow ones that grew ever more narrow as I went higher. I remember one dream in particular: I was back in college, climbing the spiral staircase of a tall brick tower. The stairs grew narrow, so much so that I felt squeezed, unstable, and afraid of falling backward. For some reason I could not turn around and go back down the stairs. Up was the only option, and it led to a perilous dead end.

This dream says something about my own struggles with temptation. One of the greatest temptations all of us face is the temptation to be like God. This one stretches all the way back to Eden, when the serpent laid out the benefits of eating from the tree of the knowledge of good and evil: "You will not die; for God knows that when you eat of it your eyes will be opened, and you will be like God" (Gen. 3:4-5). That statement clinched it: Eve wanted to be divine, and she yielded to that temptation. We humans attempt divinity by taking complete control, orchestrating our lives and the lives of others as if we were puppet masters, playing out events as we deem best.

Jesus' temptations in the wilderness also fall along these lines. First, Satan tempts him to turn stones into bread, which Jesus must have wanted, since he must have been hungry. Second, Satan suggests that he defy the laws of gravity, even defy death itself, by throwing himself off the pinnacle of the Temple. In his third and final temptation, Satan offers Jesus all the worldly power he could want, earthly omnipotence, if he will bow down and worship Satan. In summary, Jesus' three temptations present him with chances to be Godlike, to mold the physical world to suit his momentary, personal wishes. Satan tempts Jesus to gratify all his own desires, to defy his physical limitations, to take charge of the world and claim its splendor for himself—all faculties natural to God, not to human beings. Jesus, of course, refuses to reach toward omnipotence. Even as God incarnate, Jesus chooses to behave as a human being living among us. In so choosing, he remains himself and lets God be God.

When we look for our own temptations during this wilderness time, we would do well to watch for ways we try to be minigods. The Gospel lessons for Lent indicate that temptation is one of the hallmarks of wilderness time. The temptations we encounter may be of the hubris variety. Like Icarus flying toward the sun, we will be tempted to exceed our natural abilities. For example, when we sit quietly and encounter our own inner wildernesses, we may come face-to-face with temptations to make things happen: to make someone love us, to make our work follow a certain course, or to control another's life. These temptations are the very stuff that wilderness is made of, and yielding to them leads to more chaos.

Exploring the wilderness this week entails naming our temptations and being scrupulously honest with ourselves about them. We admit our tendencies to make ourselves like God. We all have these tendencies; we all sometimes depart from ourselves and try to be more than we naturally are. For instance, as a graduate student, I worry about how I will get through school, about what kind of job I'll get when I get out. Will I be able to make enough money? Will I enjoy the work? Will I have good health insurance, a comfortable home, enough income to support a family someday? The list goes on. This thinking shows me one of my temptations, the type that I find in my own personal wilderness. In essence, when I worry this way, I am overstepping myself, trying to see into the future, trying to orchestrate a safe life rather than living authentically, doing my best, and following God's guidance into the future God intends for me.

During this first week, listen for your temptations and hear what they ask. Naming the temptations does not mean either yielding to them or resisting them. You will have time in later weeks to decide how to handle all of them. For now accept that temptations are present and part of this wilderness that you courageously choose to enter.

WILD BEASTS

Recently I went backpacking with my sisters and brother. We had just started our hike up to Raven Point when a couple coming down from the point stopped us and warned, "Watch out for snakes!" They launched into a tale of two harrowing snake encounters. In the first, the woman was settling in for a lunchtime picnic on the point, and just as she started to sit, she realized that her spot was already occupied by a rattlesnake. She got up quickly, frightened but unhurt. Shortly thereafter, the two of them spotted a poisonous copperhead sunning itself on the point about thirty feet away from them. Probably still shaken by her first snake encounter, the woman extended her walking stick, picked up the snake, and flung it. The snake hit a tree, bounced off, and went over the cliff, never to be seen again. The snake-flinging part of the story held particular appeal for the storytellers and for us as wide-eyed listeners. The couple recounted the snake's bouncing off the tree several times with great zeal: "It bounced off a tree! It bounced off a tree, and then it went over the cliff!"

This episode sums up a universal human inclination toward wild beasts. We want to rid ourselves of them, sometimes with good reason. They can pose genuine threats, and we have to protect ourselves from them. The Gospel passages about Jesus' wilderness stay, however, tell us that Jesus was "with the wild beasts." He seems to have sat quietly with them. Apparently he didn't fling them anywhere.

When we enter the inner wilderness of our own lives and psyches, we also find wild beasts. Our wild beasts are simply the parts of ourselves and our worlds that we can't control. We often feel threatened by them, justifiably so. But we also tend to perceive them as threats even when they really mean us no harm.

Emotions, for instance, arise in us unbidden and can seem like wild beasts. Sometimes we can talk ourselves into or out of a feeling; but most of the time, the feeling just arises, and we choose how or if we will handle it. If we feel that a certain emotion— usually one falling into the "negative" category, such as anger, grief, or fear—threatens our life's tranquillity somehow, we may choose to fling it off a cliff, gleefully watching it ricochet off trees on the way down. It is tempting to try to kill feelings in order to regain the illusion of control, stepping carefully out of the wilderness, right back onto safe city-street pavement.

But feelings don't die as easily as snakes do, and they are just as wild. Also, the truth is, we need our feelings, even the "negative" ones, to stay human, to stay fully alive. In one of my favorite *Northern Exposure* episodes, Chris, the normally mild-mannered

DJ of the local radio station, starts stealing car stereos. In a tiny Alaska town with virtually no crime, the rash of thefts creates a major disturbance. When he is finally found out, Chris turns in all the stereos, explaining, "I didn't really want them. . . . I just thought this town needed a little wildness."

We do need a certain amount of wildness and the energy it brings. Wildness creates the energy from which art is born, from which children play, from which our passion springs. We react well when we protect ourselves and those around us from unchecked wildness, but a middle ground exists between total control and total chaos. In that middle ground, we find wildness harnessed, like a river sending its energy into a dam, not stopped but trained, used, and then set free again on the other side. Emotions, even those we consider dangerous or threatening, are forms of internal energy. Instead of muting our emotions, we can befriend them, listen to their counsel, and channel their energy toward our benefit. When I picture Jesus sitting with the wild beasts in the wilderness, I envision him communing with them. I picture him not changing their wildness but celebrating and even enjoying it. Our task as we relate to our emotions is the same: Who are these creatures? How do we usually relate to them? Have we tried to kill them? What help or friendship might they offer us?

ANGELS

In the wilderness, temptations and wild beasts tend to take center stage. They make this place what it is—disconcerting, tumultuous, and difficult. With temptations and wild beasts dancing all around, you can easily miss the presence and care of angels. As you identify temptations and beasts in the wilderness, watch for angels too; and try your best to accept their care. You will need care in the wilderness, as we all do, as even Jesus did.

As I look back at my difficult freshman year of college, I remember several angels without whom I might have been much more lost. I had a boyfriend across the country whose long-distance phone calls were my mainstays. I talked to him on the phone for hours, hunched on the hardwood floor of the hallway to my room, sitting under a single light in the darkness as my roommate slept. He urged me to take the pressure off myself, not to try so hard, to drop a class, to drop all my classes—anything to take care of myself. After a long time, I listened, but his angelic concern for my well-being meant more than any advice. He cared enough to listen and give me whatever help he could.

My parents also spent hours on the phone with me, consoling me. I listened to music like Neil Young's "After the Gold Rush," because I thought his voice sounded sad, and it made me feel less alone. Reading Thomas Merton's *No Man Is an Island* gave me a new sense of God's presence. Merton spoke about the Christian spiritual life with intelligence and conviction, and even with all my adolescent skepticism about Christianity, I thought that such a smart man couldn't be entirely wrong. Trusting in Merton's confidence, I began to believe that there was more to life than individual achievement—that in God's kingdom an entirely different set of values is at work, and that my small life might even have meaning apart from the accolades I managed to accrue.

I felt intense distress, but at the same time I found angels to help me. Somehow I managed to receive their help in the midst of my pain. Angels in the wilderness come in unexpected forms, and while they may not be all sugary sweetness, they say and do what we need for our care.

We can easily forget the angels at times, especially when our fight for survival consumes us. But this week and throughout Lent, watch for the bits of saving grace that mitigate your difficulties. They are present, as surprising and unexpected as they may be, and you can count on them to appear and reappear as needed. You are not alone in a Lenten wilderness, and your needs will be met.

REFLECTION QUESTIONS

This week is yours to map your own wilderness. If you find time each day to sit in silence, try answering the following questions quickly after each quiet session. Answering them quickly allows answers to emerge from intuition, and you can look back at the end of the week and see where intuition pointed. In a way, your answers to these questions will form a map that will help you in the weeks to come.

1. What drives you into your own wilderness?

2. What are your temptations in this place? In what ways are you tempted to overreach your human limitations?

3. Read Luke's rendition of Jesus' experience in the wilderness, in Luke 4:1-13. Move through the passage slowly, imagining yourself in Jesus' position. What images appear to you at each of "the devil's" tempting statements?

4. When you imagine a wilderness experience, what emotions stir in you?

5. What help do you have in this wilderness? Who (or what) might serve as angels to you?

WEEK 2

first clearing

Rend your hearts and not your clothing.

—Joel 2:13

Now that we know something about the wilderness, this second week becomes a time to choose a particular part of it and select a practice to clear space there. Knowing where we are driven when we sit still, and knowing the temptations and wild beasts of this place, how can we begin to create a small oasis of peace amid the chaos?

The work we do in this area will become a Lenten discipline, which follows the tradition of giving up something for Lent. We may give up something or take on a new discipline; either practice builds awareness and helps us open to God. Only you can select your best practice. Identify a project small enough to work on during the five remaining weeks of Lent. Surprisingly, much benefit can come from working only in a limited area.

The wilderness can overwhelm, so try not to clear the entire place at once, turning the whole wilderness into a giant garden. Instead, start with one small patch and trust that the little space where God comes through will create enough openness for now and will extend into greater openness later. As you choose a practice, keep in mind the image of clearing space in your life. What change would make life feel a little more open and free, more relaxed, trusting, and faithful? Think into the question some and picture the practice that would allow you more freedom and openness from several weeks to a year from now.

REND YOUR HEARTS

Although you may have chosen a limited Lenten discipline, the first efforts of this week are important. The new pattern of behavior, no matter how tiny it seems, will open you to God's presence; and this is no small matter. While the process of opening is beautiful, it can also bring heartbreak because it entails letting go of old, dear ways of doing things. If you use this season to open to God and return to God, you may experience some pain. The writer of the book of Joel understood this truth.

> Yet even now, says the LORD,
>   return to me with all your heart,
> with fasting, with weeping, and with mourning;
>   rend your hearts and not your clothing. (2:12-13)

To put it dramatically, your Lenten discipline requires breaking your heart for God.

The intensity of this second week's "heartbreak" will vary, depending on the person and the change; but it is an essential first step. Any act of creation is also an act of destruction, so as we begin to create clear space, some things must go. Thus clearing involves loss. Even if the loss means leaving behind tired defense mechanisms and old patterns, they were *our* defense mechanisms and patterns. We developed them for a reason; they served a purpose, and losing them—even if it is time to lose them—can be confusing as well as exciting and promising.

Suppose a woman wants to clear time in her busy day to pray. She wants to open up a meager fifteen minutes, but her day is packed full of office work, household chores, taking care

INDIVIDUAL EXERCISE

The map of the wilderness you created during the first week can guide your choice of a Lenten discipline. If you sat in silent meditation last week, you now know the parts of your self and life that feel chaotic, like wild beasts. You have tried to sit with them and accept their wildness. You have identified some temptations and ways in which you overextend yourself, trying to be more God than human. Consider a practice that addresses some element of the wilderness. Rather than choosing to eradicate the obstacle or the chaos that you address, imagine a practice that simply invites God into the area to heal and transform it. If I realize in my wilderness meditations that I worry excessively, my Lenten practice would not be to stop worrying immediately. Instead it might be to pray whenever I find myself worrying: "God, please help me with my worries" or "Thy will be done." No practice is too small; a practice as small as saying a one-sentence prayer once a day can hold great meaning and value.

Your chosen practice should have a few essential features. It needs to be something you can do *regularly*—either daily or weekly. Even a small amount of time will yield great benefits if it becomes a regular habit. The practice also should be *reasonable*—something you likely can continue for the remaining five weeks. If you tend to overextend yourself, be careful not to try something too large, because you may be tempted to stop the practice before the season ends. Finally, use intuition to create a practice that feels like it will create an opening in your life, the sort of opening that allows closer communion with God. If you have difficulty selecting a Lenten practice, see the appendix for suggestions.

of children, and so on. This woman's wilderness is one of extreme busyness, and she wants to clear just a small window of time to rest in God's presence. Now comes the heartbreak: something has to go. If her day was full before, she must give up something in order to make room. What will it be—a little extra time at the office? some work around the house? Relinquishing control in some of these areas may frighten her. While her losses may seem insignificant at first glance, when she removes pieces from her daily life, she glimpses what it means to break one's heart for God.

The phrase "Rend your hearts" in Joel could become the basis for an elaborate yet false display of grief, which could play into stereotypes about Lent. Lent could become a long time to act sad without touching any real sadness. It could become a big, somber production, long and tedious, full of fasting and weeping, without real substance behind it. Yet God desires depth from our work during this season, as the Joel passage implies. To "rend your hearts and not your clothing" means to make more than mere surface changes. We try to open from a deeper place, making change that goes straight to the essence of who we are. We are asked to break open a central soul-place and to reveal its emotional contents to God, in whose care these emotions are safe. Such a deep place carries grief as well as joy, pain as well as happiness. These feelings may come flooding back if they have been longing to get out for years. Or the heart may break open slowly, with some resistance, and its tender contents come flowing out like a small stream. In either case, the effect is the same: we go into a place that has been closed off and overgrown, and we voluntarily open it up, voluntarily rend our own hearts.

Psychotherapists and counselors may recognize this sort of heartbreak from another perspective, as it is generally understood that in therapy, a person begins to feel worse before he or she feels better. Therapy—or any significant experience of introspection and change—rends one's heart in the way the book of Joel describes. In therapy a person begins to clear away defenses, old habits, and destructive patterns. Underneath those patterns is the heart—the tender, vulnerable, and wounded core self. When feelings, long held at bay, begin to emerge, a person initially feels more pain than before the therapy started. This phenomenon creates confusion if the individual embarking on a therapy process doesn't expect it, because it seems that efforts to heal are making life worse. However, when one moves through long-unfelt emotions and continues with courageous change, a richer, fuller life results, producing a deeper connection with oneself and others. The initial heartbreak is a necessary part of the process, and it is the type of heart rending that our clearing Lenten work asks us to do. By clearing space, we open a tender spot that we had closed off, and we offer it to God for healing.

> When we allow our hearts to break for God's sake and we express that heartbreak openly, our vulnerability draws us into closer communion with God and others.

When such heartbreak occurs, remember that the heart breaks for God, not just for the sake of feeling pain or confusion. Pain in itself may have no particular meaning, but pain dedicated to God becomes sacred. This heartbreak, focused on opening our lives so we draw closer to God, is surely this kind of sacred heart rending.

Singer-songwriter Ashley Cleveland tells how, after one particularly disappointing breakup, she began wearing a Band-Aid on her shirt, right over her heart.[1] She wanted the world to know that her heart was broken. This seems like a good gesture for this second week of Lent. Most of us think we should hide our deep feelings because the world doesn't want to see them.

But when we allow our hearts to break for God's sake—for the sake of greater love and truth—and we express that heartbreak openly, with fasting, weeping, and mourning, our vulnerability draws us into closer communion with God and others. In Ashley Cleveland's case, the man she eventually married was drawn to the vulnerability of her broken heart. While the experience may be uncomfortable and even frightening, we gain something when we willingly open our hearts and let their contents flow out: a new opportunity to connect with one another and with God. The Lenten invitation to "rend your hearts" is not a rending just for the sake of destruction. It is a rending for the sake of greater openness, tenderness, and ultimately, for greater connection.

HONORING THE HARDENED HEART

The first step in rending one's heart for God is learning to respect and appreciate the hardened heart. We all have hardened or closed our hearts in various ways for various reasons, and we will do it again. The hardened heart is essentially a collection of defenses that protect us from harm; some of these defenses have been in place for years, others for only a little while. When first put into place, defenses serve us admirably by muting or deflecting pain.

Children are particularly creative in building defenses because often they have no other way to handle a difficult situation. For instance, the child of an alcoholic mother might become a superachiever because achieving gives her a much-needed sense of control. Perfect grades and a perfectly tidy room give her a sense of safety. She tells herself that a perfectly ordered life magically protects her from mother's unpredictability. The superachiever role safeguards her from a terrifying sense of powerlessness. For children, a good set of defenses can mean survival; it's amazing to see children's ingenuity and effectiveness.

Adults also need defenses. When we feel too weak to cope, when things are going badly, and when there aren't enough friends around to shore us up, a strong emotional defense makes us feel better. We owe our defenses a debt of gratitude; in many ways, they have kept us sane, and in some cases, they may even have kept us alive.

So defenses serve important purposes. But as we move into adulthood and become more able to protect ourselves from the world around us, defenses become less necessary, and overactive defenses can get in our way. They may become like armor around our hearts, protecting our soft centers but keeping others out; they separate our inner world from those with whom we'd like to connect, including God.

I talked recently with a friend who, like me, is working toward a master's of social work and plans to become a psychotherapist. She admitted to a thought I'd had—it's hard to be in a psychology-related field and not have a PhD. We both acknowledged that it is hard for us to work with people who call themselves Doctor, while we cannot call ourselves anything but Ms. In fact, my friend admitted that she is thinking about getting a PhD, not because she needs it or really wants to do the studies but because the degree will make her feel better. I could see exactly what she meant, and I appreciated her honesty. Our interest in PhDs is largely a defense to protect us from feelings of inferiority. Without conscious management, this defense could take over, driving us to achieve status in the world's eyes instead of focusing on the work we feel called to do.

As we begin our Lenten practice this week, we break our hearts by moving aside a few defenses and revealing the vulnerability they mask. Before we abandon our defenses and break our hearts wide open, we must express our gratitude for the defenses that have served us well. We need to honor and express thanks for the heart just as it is, with all of its current hardness. Our hearts' outer shells have protected the precious treasure of our inner selves. Only when we have expressed our thanks are we ready to break open the shells and reveal the precious vulnerability they have guarded for a long time.

NAMING ILLUSIONS

Illusions, almost invisible, provide some of the best defenses. Illusions are the untrue stories we tell ourselves about who we are and what we are doing, and they masquerade as truth. Usually illusions are not deliberate lies; we simply learned or created them and have come to believe them over the years. Because some illusions are so pervasive and long-standing, we may have trouble distinguishing between the illusory and the real.

In their simplest forms, illusions distort reality. Consider David who, as a child, believed he was the smartest person in the world. He never consciously thought this belief was true; if someone had confronted him with it, he would have said it was ridiculous. In grade school David played the role of "smart kid," believing that displaying his intelligence was the only way to get attention. He reasoned: *I make good grades, and that makes me special. I am smart; therefore I matter.* At the time, David needed to feel special to protect himself from total anonymity at school. As is true with many defenses, the illusion got a frightened child through a rough spot—a school situation in which he might have been ignored completely—and earned him some much-needed attention and approval.

Trouble began when David's illusion began to outlive its usefulness. Over the years, the smart-kid role had become so integral to his identity that it alone made him feel special. When he continued into college trying to play the "supersmart" role, all kinds of distortions started to unfold, like eddies spinning out into the world around him. To maintain his illusion David had to work ridiculously hard, especially in light of the truth that some people were smarter than he. How could he be a great physicist, a great philosopher, a great poet? He simply couldn't, and in trying, he moved farther and farther from his true self. In a way David's heart hardened; he no longer expressed his truth, the truth of his real desires and interests. His personal illusion walled him in.

To let go of an illusion, one begins by naming the illusion for what it is. Believing that he was the smartest kid got David through a difficult time in life. But eventually he recognized that when he told himself the smartest-kid story, self-deception was afoot. Just naming it—calling it an illusion—disempowers it and allows truth to flood in. By calling an illusion an illusion, one begins to distinguish it from truth and can see more clearly the person he or she truly is. One can stop driving oneself too hard, trying to live up to a role much too big for the "real me."

Illusions can also distort reality in another direction. Whereas David's childhood illusion told him he was more than he was, other illusions can tell us that we are less than we are. Imagine a girl who at age five began dance lessons. She loved them, enjoyed music and movement, and danced with wild abandon. However, her teacher told her that she had no rhythm and should give up dance. Crushed, she stopped going to class and stopped dancing completely. She told herself that she didn't want to dance. This illusion continued into adulthood as she continued to tell herself that she disliked dancing; this way she avoided engaging in an activity that would have exposed her to painful criticism. She used her illusion to shield the vulnerable, creative, exuberant part of herself from the pain she had felt as a child. But the fact remained that she operated under an illusion—one that protected her but severely limited her self-expression. And for this woman not to identify and name her illusion created a distortion. She was living a life too small for her.

By naming illusions, we unmask them; we learn to see them as they are, maybe even laugh at them a little, and let them go. As Buddhist writer Shunryu Suzuki said, "If you try to expel the delusion, it will only persist the more, and your mind will become busier and busier trying to cope with it. That is not so good. Just say, 'Oh, this is just delusion,' and do not be bothered by it."[2] We don't have to fight with our illusion-defenses. When we name them as illusions, they lose their power to control us. They stop working as defenses, and we get a little closer to breaking our hearts open. Naming our illusions brings us a little closer to revealing our true and vulnerable selves to God.

EXPRESSING EMOTIONS

Blocked emotions form another kind of defense. This defense is a simple form of protection: if you refuse to feel pain, you protect yourself from pain. End of story—or apparent end of story. While blocking feelings seems like effective self-protection at first, feelings tend to come back; like horror movie villains, they grow stronger the harder one tries to kill them. Not experiencing a feeling does not kill the feeling; it just stuffs the feeling deeper into a person, where it can harden. Once hardened, emotions sit like little pebbles blocking a flow of water; they prevent even positive emotions from moving between the heart and the world outside.

In *The Artist's Way*, Julia Cameron describes the phenomenon of the "blocked" artist, a person with natural creative gifts who, for various reasons, does not use them. The blocked person may fear using his or her gifts, thinking that being an artist would mean financial ruin, a tumultuous lifestyle, or painful failure and rejection. Unfortunately, choosing not to use one's gifts is like choosing not to experience one's emotions—the inner reality remains the same and continues to beg for expression. The obstacles preventing self-expression create distortions in the blocked person's life, leading to anger, jealousy, or unhappiness. The blocked artist may pretend that he has no desire to be an artist himself, but subconsciously he envies others' choices to do things that he himself would like to do.[3]

Emotions are much like art—both energies need expression, and if they go unexpressed, their energy remains. Unexpressed, their energy changes into something darker, murkier; something that would have flowed like water now has the consistency of tar. For those of us who dislike risk, this is bad news, because expressing ourselves always involves risk. But the good news is that when we clear away the blocks and express inner impulses, we move more freely. Expressing feelings (and creative impulses) sets us free; we become a slave to them only when we try to hide or quell them. Emotions (and art) can move through us like water moves in a stream. Only when we try to block its flow does it gain strength and fight harder to get around the obstacle.

Just this morning, a single friend talked to me about searching for a partner, and without warning she started to cry. I saw her fear, regret, and grief about her relationship history. Rather than feeling ashamed of her tears, she felt relieved to let them out; they needed to come out, and they flowed out easily and sweetly. Her tears brought release from her intense pain and isolation; with her tears she cleared away obstacles—broke her heart—and allowed her true inner life more freedom of motion. She then felt more able to cope with her situation; her feelings lost their looming intensity and became quieter companions.

Melting our blocked emotions is yet another way to break the heart open. When we offer our feelings to God, no matter what they are, the feelings become consecrated, transforming into blessings for us. We break our hearts for God and offer God the contents; God honors their contents, helps us with them, and moves them through us so that we can be free.

The psalmist knew the value of expressing feelings, as evidenced in the deep emotion running throughout the Psalms: "I am utterly numb and crushed; I wail, because of the groaning of my heart" (Ps. 38:8, Book of Common Prayer). The artistry of the Psalms is one of deep self-expression, and we can model our own expression after them. They teach us to open our hearts and let out our true feelings rather than allowing them to calcify. Fear, pain, anger—God can take all these. God wants to hear all our feelings, wants to come close to our hearts no matter what they contain. By allowing our hearts to break open even a little, we begin to live more authentically, openly, and abundantly.

ACCEPTING WEAKNESS

Our culture values strength, and we define strength in traditional American fashion: the rugged individual steps out into the frontier, battles the elements and animals, and manages to wrest prosperity from a barren land. It is an amazing story, and self-sufficiency truly is an important form of strength.

However, in focusing so much on self-sufficiency and sheer might as strength, we miss chances to honor more subtle, yet equally powerful, forms of strength. *Strength* in a Christian context can mean something entirely different; in fact, God's strength as described in Romans turns our culture's notion on its head: paradoxically, divine strength is "made perfect in weakness" (2 Cor. 12:9). What does this mean? How does weakness exemplify strength perfected?

The capacity to express vulnerability is a great human strength. We sometimes wish our vulnerabilities would disappear so we wouldn't have to worry about hiding them. Without these pesky vulnerabilities, we could convince the world that we have it all together, that we have no unsatisfied needs, that we can care constantly for others and never need care ourselves. It is hard to let people see our vulnerable parts—our fears and insecurities, our sadness and shame. To express vulnerability requires courage. Only in exercising this courage, in bravely showing our "weakness" to another, do we achieve a form of real power—the power to ask for help when needed.

Over the last few years, I have changed apartments several times and always find moving an ordeal. Before I viewed vulnerability as a strength, I didn't ask for help with moving. I moved a lot of boxes myself or asked one or two people—usually my parents—to help me. Consequently, moves that could have taken a few hours took several days or a week. As I have learned more respect for my vulnerability—my natural human limitations—I've discovered a greater power to take care of myself. Admitting that I can't move an entire apartment alone feels at first like an admission of weakness; but admitting it, I gain strength—the power to reach out for help and receive it.

Human beings need care, especially during childhood when our lives depend on it. But we also need it as adults. No one, not even the most rugged individual, is entirely self-sufficient. Christ's Good Shepherd image speaks directly to our need for care: here is the One who knows that we need care and seeks us out and provides for us.

By admitting our weakness, we take the first step toward embracing our true power, no matter how shameful we consider our weakness. Accepting our vulnerability is yet another way in which our hearts break for God. We break away the mask of false self-sufficiency and admit that we depend upon one another, that we depend upon God, that we are limited and human—weak by nature and strong by our ability to connect with others and to ask for what we need.

REFLECTION QUESTIONS

1. How has your Lenten practice made you aware of some of your defenses?

2. What are your favorite defenses? How have they protected you over the course of your life?

3. How have your defenses created a hardened heart? How have they created barriers between you and God or between you and others? How would you like them to serve you differently in the future?

4. When you feel that you are "rending your heart," how can you offer its contents to God?

5. Read Job's words in Job 42:2-6. He spoke them to God after a long period of struggle and searching. How might Job's experience resemble this week's heart rending?

rend your heart—
humble yourself before God.
becoming submissive.

WEEK 3

natural rhythms

For everything there is a season, and a time for every matter under heaven.

—Ecclesiastes 3:1

Whatever Lenten practice you have chosen, this week's task involves watching for patterns emerging in it. The rhythms of the practice become the new discipline's foundation; they teach us how to tailor disciplines to our own natures. By observing natural rhythms, we avoid imposing artificial, harsh routines on ourselves. While any discipline requires a degree of conformity and exertion, it is important not to undertake a rhythm that feels unnatural and fruitless, because a routine that does not speak to you personally will become onerous; your desire to rebel against it will render it ineffective. It is better to identify a personally meaningful rhythm of work and then commit to this natural rhythm as "discipline."

Suppose a man wants to make time in his day for prayer. Realizing that his own wilderness is a chaos of busyness without much sense of God's presence, he has chosen silent meditation time as his discipline for the season. He has "broken his heart" by noticing how his busyness serves as a defense, protecting him from feelings of loneliness or inadequacy. Having exposed these tender feelings to God, now he is ready to commit more deeply to a prayer practice.

As this practitioner's prayer discipline gets underway, he can watch for rhythms developing in it. He may find that he feels energized by praying at a certain time of day. He may also learn that certain prayer places work well for him too; sitting on the sofa seems too ordinary, while the chair by the window gives a sense of sacred space. He may also learn that particular forms of practice work well for him; for instance, the Morning Prayer liturgy from The Book of Common Prayer may help him frame prayer time, while without that structure, his mind wanders more. He may also find that his prayer space feels sacred if he lights a candle or burns incense. All of these observations constitute the natural rhythms arising in his practice.

Chaos and Emerging Order

We all have been through times when life felt chaotic. In fact, if Lent's wilderness week was an experience of wilderness for you, then you have a recent memory of an experience of chaos. Chaos can be unpleasant, but it is built into earthly existence simply because our world is unpredictable.

According to the Genesis creation narrative, the world began in chaos: "In the beginning when God created the heavens and the earth, the earth was a formless void and darkness covered the face of the deep, while a wind from God swept over face of the waters" (Gen. 1:1-2). Order emerged from this chaos at God's bidding, as God created distinctions where all had been mixed together. God first separated night and day, then sky and water, then earth and seas, and so on. Order unfolds out of chaos as God chooses.

Chaos theory postulates that seemingly unpredictable systems actually do form patterns. The usual laws of physics and chemistry cannot predict exactly what these patterns

INDIVIDUAL EXERCISE

This week, spend a few minutes each morning or evening reflecting on your practice the previous day. You may want to write down a few notes, answering the following questions:

- How did you feel when engaged in your Lenten discipline? Did you feel energized, or did the practice feel somewhat dry and dead?

- What influences affected your practice? Consider the time of day, the presence of other people, your mood, your awareness of outside obligations.

If your practice felt more dull than fully alive, use the observations gained above to adjust it the next day. If family obligations interrupted your prayer time, the next day you might do your prayer practice at work by closing your office door or finding a quiet spot for fifteen minutes at lunchtime. Play with the practice a little, changing the circumstances surrounding it.

The next evening or morning, engage in the same reflection, answering the same questions. Repeat this process of daily reflection and adjustment this week until your practice begins to feel natural and energizing.

If your practice involves giving up something, watch for new rhythms developing in the open space you've created. If you have been in the habit of watching TV each night after work and you gave that up for Lent, what activity seems to take its place? Do you find yourself reading more? spending more time with friends or family? Observe that newly opened time this week and see what is developing in it; notice what new habits are emerging.

will be; science can only observe that patterns form, that "complex, open systems pass from disordered phases to more complex stages of order."[4] Chaotic systems engage in a process of self-organization. Random environmental conditions come together occasionally to create order in the form of a funnel cloud. The emergence of order from chaos occurs over and over in nature—in patterns in the coats of animals, in the arrangement of feathers on birds, in the shapes of coastlines.

Chaos theory reminds us that order rises naturally out of disorder and that chaos itself is an important part of the order-creation process. We began Lent in chaos, allowing ourselves to experience the parts of our lives that felt disordered or out of control. From this formless void, we imitate God's creative process and begin to create order; this is the work of clearing space. Chaos theory reminds us that while our efforts are important and necessary, order naturally wells up on its own; the universe tends to create order from chaos, and by our efforts to clear space, we participate in this process. Thus the patterns of a new practice or discipline will emerge naturally, without imposition. We see ourselves as the creators, molding the new disciplines in our lives. And we are creators, but our creative act is truly the act of allowing patterns to emerge through us, letting ourselves become part of a larger order that develops in us and around us.

Importance of Rhythms and Laws in Clearing Space

"Six days shall work be done, but the seventh day is a sabbath of solemn rest, holy to the LORD" (Exod. 31:15).

The sabbath may be our best example of a rhythmic practice that clears space in human life. It stands out among the Ten Commandments, most of which talk explicitly about our relating to others and to God. Compared with the relational goals of the other commandments, the purpose of sabbath observance seems a little more ambiguous. Why this rhythm of sabbath time? Why should we rest regularly instead of waiting until we feel tired?

It is up to us to care for our spiritual lives with rhythmic effort.

The inclusion of sabbath observance in the Ten Commandments indicates the importance of rhythm. Sabbath centers the lives of individuals and the life of the community that the commandments were designed to protect. The sabbath protects individuals from fatigue, even burnout, and its regularity sets a predictable time for a community to come together. Communities separate to work during the week, but on the one day they are not allowed to work, they find themselves spending time together, being together as family and community. Without the sabbath rhythm, not only might individuals work beyond their true capacities but also communities might never come together. Shared rhythm protects individuals from exhaustion and communities from disintegration.

The sabbath commandment also teaches us that regular patterns are part of the divine plan for our spiritual lives. Without rhythms for clearing space in our lives, things become overgrown; the wilderness encroaches in an uncontrolled and destructive way, and our spiritual lives, both as individuals and as communities, begin to break down. As with tending a garden, the work of clearing space requires regularity. A garden is not tended in a single work session; it needs regular attention, consistency, and dependability from its caretaker. Likewise, it is up to us to care for our spiritual lives with rhythmic effort. We build structures into our lives to ensure that our cleared space will stay clear and not become overgrown.

DEVELOPING RHYTHMS: LAW VERSUS GRACE

Laws and rhythms structured ancient Hebrew culture, forming the basis for Jewish religious practice. Christianity is grounded in the same laws, which serve as moral precepts and as shared commitments that have held communities together for thousands of years. Together these laws create a structure in which human beings can work and live together; they create harmony among human beings and between human beings and God.

According to Jesus' summary of the commandments, love is the basis for law. After hundreds of years of communal Ten Commandment observance, Jesus said that he could summarize all the laws with just two commandments: "'You shall love the Lord your God with all your heart, and with all your soul, and with all your mind.' This is the greatest and first commandment. And a second is like it: 'You shall love your neighbor as yourself.' On these two commandments hang all the law and the prophets" (Matt. 22:37-40). In giving this summary, Jesus says to his listeners: The essence of the laws we follow is love—for God and one another—and we must enact the laws from this essence to follow them truly. What matters most is not our detailed, pious observance of the law but the heart with which we fulfill them.

This conversation between the letter and spirit of the law is also seen in Christian tradition as the "law versus grace" debate. In Romans we read that Christ's sacrifice sets us free from the law: "You are not under law but under grace" (Rom. 6:14). Grace rescues us from the law's harsh judgments; it promises God's unfailing love to humankind. Living by grace means that we live by love; the law, when used well, serves the larger purpose of renewing love in the world.

The tension between law and grace illuminates our Lenten effort to build rhythms into developing practices. On the one hand, our changes need discipline; they need externally imposed laws to get started. On the other hand, for a practice to be authentic and lasting, it needs to arise from within—from a true, deep place of love and commitment. When made from love and grace, changes have an inner truth; they resonate in service of the life they impact.

Law and grace work together over time. Suppose a person wishes to clear time to improve her physical health during Lent; she commits to a discipline of walking for thirty minutes each morning. At first the woman must rely on the law: she has to force herself to arise thirty minutes earlier each morning, get dressed, get out the door, and take those first few sluggish steps. Maybe she even needs a walking partner, someone to call her at 6:00 AM and tell her to get out of bed. These first efforts are a legalistic way to start clearing space in her life. She forces herself to stick with her new routine.

At the same time, if grace does not come into play, the discipline will not serve its purpose. If a love for walking does not begin to grow in the woman's heart through faithfulness to her discipline, eventually she will abandon it, and it will not serve its true purpose of improving her health. Without a love welling up and reinforcing the discipline, eventually the discipline will fail. This love is a form of grace—it arises in us unbidden; it is out of our control, and, in this sense, it is a gift from God, a gift of grace.

Law and grace repeatedly balance each other, challenge each other, and push the practitioner of the discipline to ever deeper engagement with the discipline itself. As in the example above, sometimes the woman will be so inspired by her walking practice that getting out the door seems almost effortless. She can picture her walk before she begins and see herself on a quiet street with trees curving in overhead. She sees herself blissfully alone and moving, with the smell of dew-soaked earth and crisp early-morning air all around her, and she has all the motivation she needs to begin.

But some days, weeks, and months the woman will find every excuse not to walk. She tells herself that she could use the time to clean house, pay bills, catch up on reading. At this point, the law becomes her friend again; it steps in where grace is temporarily lacking, saying, "No excuses; just start walking." And gradually, with discipline, her love for walking returns.

At times change is easy; at other times it is difficult. Discovering a natural rhythm means listening to these shifts, allowing them to happen, and balancing law and grace as needed.

LISTENING

Our lives have their own rhythms, and we can recognize them if we listen for them. Circadian rhythms provide a good example of natural life-rhythms. The line between "night people" and "morning people" can be quite distinct. As children, my sister and I shared a room, and she hardly ever fell asleep at bedtime. I, on the other hand, dropped off right after we said good night. Through college, Annie thought nothing of staying up late, pulling all-nighters to write papers, while I despised being up all night and felt miserable when I had to do it. Even now, when our family goes on vacation, Annie stays up past midnight, enjoying the quiet, and I am in bed by ten o'clock. I do my best work in the morning, while she still does best at night. We did not learn these habits; we grew up with the same rules, the same bedtimes, and the same basic daily routines. Our body chemistries seem to dictate different daily rhythms for us.

Our prayer habits, or any regular practice we engage in, may have similar natural rhythms. Certain rhythms are hardwired into us, and it helps to discover what ours are. By finding our natural patterns, we engage our deepest selves in our practice.

So how do we know what practices are right for us? It isn't always easy to tell; determining the right practices may require experimentation. Vacations and retreats are good times to experiment, because life's usual structures are temporarily dismissed, and one's body and mind can fall into patterns that feel natural. Without an alarm clock, you find out when your body naturally wakes up; you eat when you want, engage in physical activity when you want, and spend time with others when you want. This kind of retreat experiment, while a luxury, is also a good investment of energies. Thus one can find one's rhythms and gradually build them into daily life.

On a recent beach vacation, I found out that I liked to go to bed at 11:00 PM and wake up at 8:00 AM. Sadly, I have not been successful in building this rhythm into my life back home. I rarely get a chance—or create space, perhaps—for nine hours of sleep. But now I know where I gravitate, and I can mindfully create space for at least eight hours of sleep per night. I also noticed that I feel energized by praying in the morning and journaling at night. When I tried to journal in the morning and pray at night, the practices yielded less engagement.

In distinguishing your own best practice patterns, the real crux of the matter is this: What patterns yield a sense of simultaneous energy and peace? What rituals bring more light into your life? In what rhythms do you feel closest to God?

STRUGGLE

Some struggle is natural as we work to clear space; it is work, after all, and sometimes work proves difficult. The book of Romans has much to say about struggle in the spiritual life: "I do not do what I want, but I do the very thing I hate. . . . I delight in the law of God in my inmost self, but I see in my members another law at war with the law of my mind, making me captive to the law of sin that dwells in my members" (7:15, 22-23). Even when we know what we want to do, we sometimes fail to do it. This inner conflict can feel as intense as Paul's battle between the law of God and the law of sin. Beginning a new spiritual practice is not easy, nor is it easy to stick with it.

Alan Jones, dean of Grace Cathedral in San Francisco, has said that there are two basic emotions: love and fear. These two poles illuminate Paul's struggle between the law of God and the law of sin: if the law of God is love, then the law of sin might be fear. Jesus says again and again, "Do not be afraid." When telling his listeners not to worry, reassuring them that they will be provided for just as birds and lilies are, he says, "Do not be afraid, little flock, for it is your Father's good pleasure to give you the kingdom" (Luke 12:32). When a storm hits the boat in which he and his disciples are traveling, they awaken him in hopes that he can save them. Jesus responds, "Why are you afraid? Have you still no faith?" (Mark 4:40). When Jairus hears that his daughter is dead, Jesus responds, "Do not fear. Only believe, and she will be saved" (Luke 8:50).

Jesus thus illuminates an opposition between fear and faith, fear and the kingdom, fear and belief. All these polarities manifest the struggle between fear and love, a primal struggle that pervades human existence. We cannot truly love—or have faith or set our hearts on God's kingdom—when consumed by fear. Fear overrides all other thoughts and feelings, and self-preservation becomes our primary objective, making it impossible for us to attend to others' needs in a loving, faithful way.

How do we vanquish fear? Like other emotions, fear seems to grow stronger the harder we try to push it down. I have experienced firsthand the resilience of fear: I am terrified of public speaking and have found that the more I deny my fear, the stronger it gets. Life has offered me plenty of blessed public speaking opportunities, and I have learned ways to handle my fear. Every time I have to give a talk, the pattern is the same. As I sit waiting for my turn to speak, I try to concentrate, but my mind goes in and out of contact with the world around me. I try turning my thoughts toward my talk, but they move inward, toward my panic. At this point, I usually feel a strong desire to run. I can imagine the whole scenario: I see myself jumping up suddenly, without explanation, and fleeing the room, never to return. I weigh the feasibility of this option. It seems pretty reasonable until I picture the embarrassment I'd feel about ten minutes after leaving the room. I reluctantly dismiss the idea. Thus I remain, panicking in my chair, and my feelings of fear grow more and more intense until the moment I actually stand up and walk toward the podium. I always make it through the talk, but my voice shakes, and sometimes I lose my train of thought.

My fear is strongest when it becomes a monster to me. Before I talk, I usually try to tell myself I am not afraid, that nothing is wrong, that I feel confident and happy to be speaking. I treat my fear as a monster to be quashed, believing I can kill it by ignoring it. In essence, I spend the time before my talk trying to hide my fear from myself and my audience, hoping that if I deny it, it will go away.

Recently I tried a different strategy as I gave a presentation to a professor and two fellow students. I recognized my usual desire to run. But instead of hiding my feelings, I chose to tell my small audience how nervous I was. Because it was a small, friendly group, they handled it beautifully, reassuring me of their support. I then gave my presentation exactly as I had wanted, managing to think clearly and creatively and convey all my ideas.

In my presentation that day, I took a step toward befriending my fear. Paradoxically, the struggle between love and fear is won when we stop struggling. When I accepted fear and chose not to hide it in shame but to share it with others, it lost its power over me, becoming one small part in the overall experience of my presentation.

When we struggle in our new practice, it is important to make friends with the practice's would-be enemies: fear, laziness, anxiety, and the restless mind. When Jesus says, "Do not be afraid," he does not advise us to shut ourselves off to fear. He urges that we learn to set fear to one side, thereby putting the kingdom first. We can set aside fear when we acknowledge its presence, learn any lessons it might give us, and then assign it an appropriate supporting role in our lives. As your rhythmic practice develops this week, try to welcome points of struggle. They offer an opportunity to befriend your practice's enemies, to meet a part of yourself that may have been ignored or undervalued. As you befriend this one-time enemy, the struggle abates, and you can direct more of your energy toward love.

GENTLENESS

When developing a disciplined practice, one of the most valuable gifts we can give ourselves is gentleness. In everyday life, we tend to associate discipline with rigidity, rules, and consequences for misbehavior. Sometimes this kind of discipline is indeed necessary. However, we tend to downplay the equally important role of gentleness in making changes. Change requires a great deal of effort from anyone engaged in it, even if the change is positive. Change plunges a previously ordered system into temporary chaos, and chaos is stressful. Gentleness takes into account our effort and stress; treating ourselves gently is a way of offering encouragement and appreciation for the work being done.

Being gentle with ourselves may not come naturally. Many of us, accustomed to using punishment to reinforce discipline, forget gentleness as an option. Those of us who forget to be gentle with ourselves need to consciously cultivate a gentle inner voice. We can learn to speak in a gentle manner to ourselves, asking how the work is going and then listening carefully to our own answers.

Speaking and listening with gentleness is much harder than we would think. It is easier to talk to ourselves harshly and ignore the hurt feelings that result. Sometimes a lopsided inner dialogue sounds like drill sergeant orders: "Get up! Get to work! Stop loafing! You're going to be late!" And so on. A conscious, gentler inner dialogue might begin by asking questions instead: "Why don't you want to get up? Are you too tired? Why don't you want to go to work? Do you need more rest?" Further gentle treatment would mean listening carefully to the answers to these questions.

Gentleness requires a commitment to not judge or criticize our own answers in this dialogue process. When Jesus said, "Do not judge, and you will not be judged" (Luke 6:37), I think he meant that quite literally. When we mete out judgments and criticisms, we eventually become targets of our own assault. The critical inner voice is hard to control. When active within us, it is directed inward as easily as outward. By cultivating gentleness, we begin to speak the truth to ourselves in love, and this compassionate response furthers our discipline more than any criticism.

REFLECTION QUESTIONS

1. What rhythms are developing in your Lenten practice? What changes have you noticed according to times of day, locations, and other external circumstances?

2. How does your own nature gravitate toward a particular rhythm?

3. In what ways do you notice law and grace contributing to your continued practice? When have you had to force yourself to continue a spiritual practice? When have you felt so inspired that force was unnecessary?

4. Read Psalm 19, considering its celebration of the law: "The law of the LORD is perfect, reviving the soul" (v. 7). How does your obedience to the "law" of your practice revive your soul?

WEEK 4

new growth

I am about to do a new thing; now it springs forth,
do you not perceive it?

—Isaiah 43:19

Even in the midst of Lent, moments of new life and growth
occur. The season requires discipline and work, but the benefits
of the work begin to manifest themselves even while the work is
underway. This week we will look for new growth in cleared
spaces, as the spaces begin their transformation into gardens.

Rather than bursting at once into full flower, new growth
comes up tiny and vulnerable. The attentive Lenten observer
watches for it carefully, because it needs protection and care.
The first step this week is to learn what we are looking for.
What signs indicate that we are moving closer to God? Among
the possible signs are increased creativity, a strengthened capacity to love, and greater openness to surprise. As you observe
yourself this week, watch for new creative impulses, which
demonstrate that your work has opened creative channels. Pay
attention to any newfound abilities to express care for others.
Also notice how you react to surprises and spontaneity. Any
changes in these areas may result from a Lenten discipline of
opening and clearing.

The next step for the week is to provide the nurture this new growth needs so it can continue to grow and flourish. There is no need to force anything; with the work of clearing and tending, growth happens on its own. All we have to do is create the right conditions for our inner lives to expand and flourish. We create those conditions through gratitude and celebration.

I have tried sporadically to learn to play the guitar; for a few weeks at a time, I make time in my day to practice. When I begin learning a new song, it initially sounds like a loose collection of notes, related only by their temporal closeness to one another. But if I persist in practice, playing the same song day after day, the notes eventually coalesce into something that sounds like music. When I have practiced long enough and consistently enough, my work starts to pay off, and I find that I am not just playing the right chords; I am playing a song. The moment at which notes become a song is like the moment our Lenten discipline yields growth. At such a moment, one's practice takes on a life of its own; it begins to feel natural, and its benefits outweigh the difficulties surrounding the practice. Just as my songs need more practice before I play them, so new growth in a Lenten practice needs more attention and work. But growth is occurring, and it is worth taking time to notice and celebrate it.

SIGNS OF NEW GROWTH: CREATIVITY

One manifestation of new growth is a stronger inclination toward creativity. As we open ourselves by successfully clearing space in our lives, creative energy flows more easily. Thus the new growth that you find in this week may manifest itself as tiny creative impulses. New growth may arise in you in the impulse to do something new.

Isaiah gives us guidance about holy creativity: "Do not remember the former things, or consider the things of old. I am about to do a new thing; now it springs forth, do you not perceive it? I will make a way in the wilderness and rivers in the desert" (43:18-19). Out of the wilderness where we started, God has begun to do a new thing in us; God's creativity springs forth through us, giving life and sustenance in a dry land.

I once thought that creativity involved making something, with the verb "to make" being akin to the verb "to force." Being creative meant that you forced something into existence—that artists used their reason and powers to choose a subject and make a product out of that subject. In my view of creativity, a sculptor would force clay into the shape he or she decided it should take. The decision, in this case, is based on the sculptor's rational and individual choice; personal whim, fashion, or even a school assignment could dictate what form the clay should take. In this model of creativity, the creator, like a god, rationally decides what to create and how to create it.

I have since come to think of creativity differently. Now I believe that all human beings are artists; we all see the world differently and have different gifts for expressing what we see. Creativity is natural; it doesn't have to be forced. We are creative because we share God's Creator nature, made as we are in God's image. All we have to do is open ourselves to divine creativity, and inspiration comes. According to this view, we don't really choose what to create; rather, inspiration chooses us as its vehicles. We are instruments of God in the world, and opening ourselves to our creativity allows us to act in greater harmony with God's will for us. This removes some of the pressure when we want to "be creative"; we don't have to act as isolated, independent agents, laboriously choosing products to create. We are vehicles, open conduits for God's creativity naturally flowing through us.

Through some clearing work, this natural inner creativity may begin to emerge. Just as new growth is small, our creative impulses may be small. My own creative impulses are as small as a desire to cook dinner. I normally eat quick pasta meals or frozen dinners. But when I slow down my life a little, stop packing it full of work and engagements and create some free time, I find that I actually want to cook for fun. And when I do cook, creative energy extends further outward into my life. I create more than a single meal; I create a warmer home for myself and a healthier body, and I wind up with more relaxed attention to give other work. Listening to that one small creative impulse—to make dinner—activates a creative chain reaction.

Creativity, then, is essentially a matter of listening, seeing, paying attention, and expressing what we hear, see, and notice to those around us. Our work in this season may pay off in greater creativity by cultivating greater openness. We open ourselves to our own inner worlds, which contain treasure chests of insights, wisdom, and knowledge; and our new growth may manifest itself in a creative desire to express what we find.

There is nothing forced about this creative growth; you are simply making room and God is doing new things in you.

If you feel unsure of your creativity, be patient. Continue your practice. Rest assured that you are a child of God, and God's energy flows through you just as it flows through every living thing.

SIGNS OF NEW GROWTH: LOVING

Another sign of new growth is a growing capacity to love. Loving is not easy, not nearly as easy as being loved. As Erich Fromm points out, "People believe that *to love* is simple but that *to be loved* is most difficult. In our [culture's] marketing orientation, people think they are not loved enough because they are not 'attractive' enough. . . . They do not know that the real problem is not the difficulty of being loved but the difficulty of loving."[5] The work of loving resembles our Lenten work of clearing space or tending a garden; it is not accomplished in one great effort but is a daily, regular responsibility. We need practice to learn to do it well.

As we grow spiritually and new life springs up in us, we discover that we have more love to give, and we feel more confident in our giving. New growth increases our sense of being filled, and we begin to engage in the activity of loving from a place of abundance. Our growth includes the assurance that giving will not leave us utterly depleted, that there will be more love where that came from. By doing our inner work this season, we discover that we have deep wells of love capacity in us, capacity that comes from God, and these wells never run dry. This is like the living water that Jesus tells the Samaritan woman about, the water that means we never need fear being thirsty.

In loving well we give of ourselves to foster another's growth or well-being. We do not discover our capacity to love by rationally deciding, *I will give all this away and know that my well will be filled again.* But spiritual growth, the kind of new growth we may experience this season, leads to a felt understanding of our deep capacities. Through a process of self-opening, the truth of one's loving capacity moves from head knowledge to heart knowledge, where we begin to feel the abundantly loving spirit instinctively. We know from our heart, not our head, that resources are plentiful.

I have long subsisted with a feeling of scarcity, always inclined to worry. Oddly enough, worrying makes me a feel that I have situations under control, that all the potential threats are named, located, and covered. Nothing will surprise me, because I know what's coming; I even know what has a 1 percent chance of coming. I am ready for anything.

I take some measure of comfort in the feeling of preparedness that worry gives me. The only trouble is that this feeling is based on a falsehood: it distorts reality in favor of fear, not love. As spiritual growth happens, I learn more deeply what Jesus means when he says, "Do not worry about your life, what you will eat, or about your body, what you will wear" (Luke 12:22). In new growth I begin to experience safety in trusting God; by deeper spiritual practice, I begin to observe that my needs really will be met. Then I am free to set my heart on the kingdom; I am free to love.

Not long ago I was frantically busy, worrying about a school project and responsibilities to a group I was leading. It was also my mother's birthday. I knew my mom would be satisfied with a phone call on her birthday. I felt so busy; I had so much that I "had" to do, so many tasks that worried me.

Instead of making the phone call, I stopped by my mom's house and gave her flowers. When I recall that day, visiting her is the only part of it that I remember. I don't remember how the school project went or what happened with my group. But I remember going to a floral shop and asking the florist to put together a bouquet, and I remember its bright summer colors. I remember laying the bouquet on the seat of my car and driving to my mom's house. And I remember how surprised and happy she was to see me.

Some tiny gift of new growth in me allowed me to set aside my usual worries, to have faith that all would be fine, and then to reach out in love. If you feel inclined to give during this season, take it as a sign of increased capacity for love. Your practice has nurtured new growth in you, and it deserves to be celebrated.

SIGNS OF NEW GROWTH: OPENNESS TO SURPRISE

Another good indicator of new growth is openness to surprises. As Brother David Steindl-Rast has put it, the essence of gratitude is saying to God, "Surprise me." A willingness to be surprised is a matter of trust in God, of trusting that somehow God's surprises are always good.

A few weeks ago I was driving at rush hour along a route I have driven hundreds of times. I hardly notice the road anymore; sometimes I reach my destination and realize that I can't remember a single detail about the drive because my mind was utterly elsewhere. On this particular day, I stopped at a red light, and I happened to glance over at the grocery store to my right. Standing next to the bushes alongside the store was a full-grown deer. It looked majestic yet absolutely strange in that suburban neighborhood. It was a powerful glimpse of natural beauty, serene and wild, standing next to a grocery store along a four-lane highway.

For some reason, that glimpse woke me up. My mind made contact with the present moment again, jarred out of its reverie by unexpected beauty. I was given a generous reminder that surprises happen all the time, even when we think we are just traveling from point A to point B in five o'clock traffic.

Many such incidents occur each day, but we notice only some of them. If we remain open to surprise, we tend to notice more of them. The universe constantly gives us little gifts, little clues about ourselves and our lives, little bits of guidance, little gifts of inspiration. And as we grow spiritually, we open more to possibilities; we look for the gifts we are being given instead of the successes and failures of our own plans. We say to God, "Surprise me."

God's surprises are like those of the pregnancy stories in the Bible. Mary's pregnancy is certainly unexpected, as is that of her cousin Elizabeth, who was believed to be barren. In Genesis, Sarah is told in her old age that she will have a child, and she laughs. The idea seems utterly absurd to her. These pregnancies reflect God's type of surprise, which makes the impossible real.

In common parlance, we talk of good and bad surprises— those that benefit us and those that do not. Are these pregnancies good surprises for the women involved? As readers of the Bible, we believe that they are good, because we know the great gain of humankind. But this surprising news might have terrified Mary. For her the surprise might have meant social ostracism and great difficulty. Still, she said to God, "Let it be with me according to your word" (Luke 1:38). She opened herself to God's surprise, regardless of its impact on her own life. This openness to surprise signals spiritual growth. By such openness we say to God, "Whatever you give me, whatever surprise comes to me from you, I accept and welcome."

Thus we shift in our attitudes toward surprise: spiritual growth means learning to expect and welcome surprise of any kind. The hard part of this growth process comes in accepting that we are not in control. This season, as we clear space, we allow new things to happen, things that we do not entirely plan or control, things that are born of God. Even our spiritual growth may take a surprising form, because it is not of our creation. It has its own nature and timing, born of God. Our challenge in saying "surprise me" means accepting that we are not always in control.

You may identify your new growth by looking at your attitude toward surprises, and you can further your growth process by praying, "Surprise me." Watch for anything unexpected in your days this week. You may tend to overlook surprises, but make a special effort to pay attention to them. They may have something to teach you; they may be gifts waiting to be opened.

> Spiritual growth means learning to expect and welcome surprises of any kind.

STRENGTH IN VULNERABILITY

When Paul tells of his "thorn in the flesh" in 2 Corinthians, he says that he first begged God to take it from him. His request is met with a paradoxical response: "My grace is sufficient for you, for power is made perfect in weakness" (2 Cor. 12:8). I wonder if Paul was thrown by the strange association—God's power located in human weakness. How can this be?

We live in a culture that celebrates physical strength and worldly power. TV and movies are full of stories in which the hero triumphs by force, using physical strength, brandishing powerful weapons. Whether we want them to or not, these images pervade our culture and make their way into our minds. Unless we challenge the culture's understanding of power, we easily begin to believe in it and even live by it. We begin to regard physical force as synonymous with power, and we want to increase our strength and come out on the winning side.

Not only does our culture celebrate power, but our own personal experiences of weakness can teach us that vulnerability makes it easy for others to take advantage of us. After being hurt, we may take away a dangerous lesson: put up a good front; let others know that you are tough and powerful, or else you'll get hurt. Vulnerability truly goes unappreciated, and worse, it is sometimes taken advantage of. Most people can recall an experience of being vulnerable that left them hurt, and we easily start to think that our vulnerability was the problem. If we just avoid showing our weaknesses, we can avoid hurt in the future.

Yet Paul offers the opposite lesson: "I will boast all the more gladly of my weaknesses, so that the power of Christ may dwell in me" (2 Cor. 12:9). He notes his own wish for his weakness to be taken from him, and then, listening to God, he changes his mind and runs in the opposite direction, shouting about his weakness from the rooftops. He has grasped God's countercultural lesson—that true strength is found in vulnerability. For Christians, power is not what the world says it is; rather, we find power in the story of the Crucifixion. We find power in a love that triumphs by passing through the vulnerability of death. Each time that force seems to have defeated the vulnerable, resurrection is actually right around the corner. Love returns to the world every time, with tender vulnerability so powerful it is unstoppable.

Vulnerability triumphs over force because it gives force nothing to fight against. A Buddhist story captures the power of vulnerability. An army had just overtaken a city, and the army's general entered the temple where a monk sat meditating. The general threatened to kill the monk if he refused to abandon the temple. The monk, unmoved by the general's threats, continued his meditation practice. Infuriated, the general said to the monk, "Don't you know who I am? I am the one who can run you through without batting an eye!" The monk responded, "And I am one who can be run through without batting an eye." The general turned and left.

Martin Luther King Jr. and Gandhi armed themselves with this sort of strong vulnerability. Their postures of nonviolent resistance ultimately won some of the most formidable battles of the twentieth century. They triumphed over great worldly powers by convincing large numbers of people to make them-selves vulnerable, to sit in silence, no matter how much they wanted to fight. Their power was indeed perfected in weakness; they used vulnerability to spread their message, gaining the attention of the entire world.

These examples do not ease the difficulty of being vulnerable ourselves. Vulnerability and weakness are always risky, even in the smallest degrees. In this week of fragile new growth, we may discover parts of ourselves that feel weak. New habits, behaviors, and patterns may make us feel unsteady and vulnerable, like toddlers taking first steps. We may feel foolish, wobbling and falling, trying to do what others already do well.

In times of wobbling and falling, remember that you are, in those very moments, allowing the power of Christ to dwell in you—the power of the same Christ who saved the world by dying a thief's death, naked and alone. Remember that vulner-ability is strength. Your comfort with your vulnerability gives you the freedom to try new things, to express yourself fully, to live in ever-expanding circles. Your tiny new growth, in all its fragility, brings a little more Christ-power into the world. So celebrate your vulnerability this week as a manifestation of great courage and strength.

REFLECTION QUESTIONS

1. What creative impulses, however small, have you felt since Lent began?

2. In what ways have you noticed yourself expressing care for others since Lent began?

3. What surprises have you experienced during this sea-son? How did you feel about them? How did you feel about surprises before the season started?

4. When have you benefited from showing your vulnerability to another?

5. Read Psalm 92, focusing on verses 12-15. What would it mean for you to be "planted in the house of the LORD" and to "flourish in the courts of our God"? In what concrete ways would such rootedness change your life?

Week 5

weathering storms

I will put my law within them, and I will write it on
their hearts.

—Jeremiah 31:33

Setbacks are a normal, healthy part of any personal change
process. They may happen unexpectedly and may even cause
disruptions. Sometimes growth feels like the proverbial "one
step forward, two steps back." In such moments of discouragement, we need to remember that setbacks can actually further
our growth. They deepen our commitments, draw us into more
intimate relationships with our fellow human beings as we
share our struggles, remind us of our natural dependence on
God's help, and teach us self-forgiveness.

At the outset of any period of change, we like to believe
that our work will go forward in tidy, linear fashion. We decide
to start exercising, and we picture ourselves waking up every
morning and heading straight to the gym, keeping to our discipline faithfully each day, now and forever. This positive
vision has its merits; it gives us hope and motivation to set us
on the new path.

For a while our image of the perfect discipline holds true.
We manage to get up every day for a week, a few weeks, even

months, and exercise as planned. Then something happens: maybe we hit a busy week at work, or our family experiences a crisis, or we tire of the routine. At this point we lose the regularity we were so proud of. We miss a few workout days, and discouragement sets in. Maybe we even feel tempted to give up, thinking that we can't keep the rhythm anymore.

Naturally we hope to make decisive, clean change, while knowing that most change in human lives gets messy. On the one hand, aiming toward perfection is admirable; we can envision the ideal and aspire to it. At the same time, when we consider our natural human limitations, such lofty goals seem strange and even a little bit funny. Rarely do human beings achieve perfection. I wonder sometimes if we amuse God with our straining and striving, trying to do everything just right.

Human beings progress in fits and starts. I experienced a long period of fits and starts when I learned to play Ultimate Frisbee a few years ago. I had never played team sports growing up, at least not in any way that felt positive or fun. So it took a friend's repeated encouragement to get me to try this sport, which requires real skills and endurance. During my first year of playing in our summer league, I must have looked like a dazed bird running around the field, moving as fast as I could but with no idea what I was supposed to do. After the summer was over, having learned very little and still barely able to handle my embarrassment on the field, I stopped playing. I would have walked away from the sport completely, but I liked the people and wanted to see them again. So I decided on a compromise: I would skip the games and show up only for the parties. This strategy worked for a while, but after listening to a lot of party conversations about games I hadn't played or even witnessed, I started to feel like a hanger-on. I totally depended on my involved friends to keep me in the community. This was no good. I needed first-hand involvement.

Set backs on our purpose, + our desire to continue can help us to focus on in the process.

I dragged myself kicking and screaming back to playing the sport. Learning meant enduring one painful, humiliating missed catch after another, but I gradually improved to a level that I could live with. I settled into a consistent rhythm and started to feel like a full member of the community. And my setback—the time I spent not playing—helped me learn how much I wanted to participate; it made me want to do the work and take the risks required to get involved.

Setbacks are always unexpected and frustrating, even if we know that they constitute a normal part of change. But with each setback, we learn and we find new opportunities to deepen our commitment to change. Each setback offers a moment for reflection. In that moment we hit a crossroads: we can choose to continue our work or not. Our choosing to continue reflects strong belief in the work's value and the rightness of our choice. And with each setback, our faith can also receive a gift if we rediscover the deep need for God made evident by our human missteps.

RENEWED COMMITMENT

The goal of Lent is not to make a plan for change and follow it to the letter. Rather, the goal is to make a change that sinks deeply into life, drawing us closer to self, others, and God. Lent is about intentionally opening ourselves, preparing to receive God's goodness. As hard as it may be to imagine, setbacks bring us closer to this goal; they take our practice to a deeper level.

This deepening of practice is much like a move from head to heart, from rational commitment to complete conviction. The book of Jeremiah describes such a shift in Israel's relationship to God's law: "This is the covenant that I will make with the house of Israel after those days, says the LORD: I will put my law within them, and I will write it on their hearts; and I will be their God, and they shall be my people" (Jer. 31:33). In this shift, the law is no longer something that the people rationally consider and obey; it carries deeper import. The law now resides in the people themselves, at their very centers. It is embedded in the place from which they make all their decisions, before

---

INDIVIDUAL EXERCISE

Consider a time this season when your practice has faltered. (If you have had no setbacks, think of any mistake you have made.) As if watching a movie, imagine yourself making the mistake or slipping in your practice. See all the circumstances surrounding the event—your state of mind at the time, any pressures you felt or difficulties you experienced. Next, fast-forward to a scene in which you see your regret about the slip.

What would you normally say to yourself upon seeing your regret? You may not be aware of any explicit statements, but try to make any unconscious self-statements conscious. Write down some of these self-statements, which could be negative or judgmental, such as "How could you do that?" or "You should be ashamed of yourself."

After writing any judgmental self-statements, acknowledge the ways in which these statements tried to protect you from the pain of repeating your mistake. Now carefully craft new statements that offer understanding and forgiveness, such as "I can see why you did that" or "I see all that happened, and I forgive you." Finally, imagine saying the forgiving statements to yourself as you picture the moment of regret. Visualize God's loving presence as you speak these new statements. Repeat the forgiving words regularly until you feel a sense of release or completion.

---

thought, at the level of preconscious knowing. This is the kind of shift we hope for this Lent, and setbacks can actually help us get there.

When I first started a regular practice of running—just thirty minutes at a time, three times a week—I really lacked commitment. When I was busy, I forgot to run, sometimes for a week at a time. I began as a casual jogger. Running wasn't my priority; I did it if I could find the time. As my practice became more regular, however, I began to notice that I felt different when I missed a week of running. My legs ached slightly— not enough to hurt but enough to let me know that my muscles wanted something from me. I talked to my sisters, also casual runners, and found that they felt the same way when they went a week without running. And we shared the same feeling about the leg aches: we hated them. Their torment constantly reminded us of what we had not been doing. We could almost feel the muscles in our legs begin to atrophy.

I haven't felt that particular ache in a long time, but I remember it, and the memory alone keeps me running. My weeklong lapses deepened my commitment to the practice, possibly enough to keep me running for a lifetime. The setbacks had real power, more than one would expect a setback to have, more than any rationalizing or convincing that my mind can conjure. When I try to maintain my discipline by reason alone, I find that I can concoct great counterarguments. But one thought of a week without running and the accompanying aches, and I can't get my running shoes on fast enough.

Every reversal we experience in moving to a new discipline offers a chance to deepen our commitment to the discipline, because it gives us opportunity to remember why we started the discipline in the first place. When we stop a new practice, we discover how much it has added to our lives, how much it has changed us, and how little we wish to return to the way things were before. We can easily beat ourselves up after mistakes, criticizing our lack of dedication or grieving over the progress that seems to be lost. But all is not lost. In fact, we gain something by losing our way: the drive to find our way back. We begin to fall in love with the practice, and it becomes part of us. It can take root and grow in the space we have cleared.

OUR NEED FOR NEIGHBORS

Often it takes a moment of crisis to wake us up to our need for others, making us aware of the interdependence that is a natural part of being human. When things are going well, we tend to live an illusion of independence, not only from God but also from our fellow human beings. As long as life moves smoothly forward, we tend to think we can handle everything on our own. However, a passing storm—any kind of setback or crisis—reminds us that we need help.

In an effort to understand Jesus' teachings about love, a listener asks, "Who is my neighbor?" (Luke 10:29). It's a good question, and a fundamental one if we hope to follow Christ. If loving neighbor is one of the great commandments of our faith, we need to know who our neighbor is. The English word *neighbor* fails to capture the depth of the relationship Jesus describes. In Jesus' teaching, our neighbor is not just the person we wave to on the way to pick up the newspaper in the morning but the stranger upon whom our very lives depend.

In his usual poetic fashion, Jesus responds to his listener's question ("Who is my neighbor?") with a story. A man traveling alone is robbed, beaten, and left on the side of the road. Two men—a priest and a Levite, prominent members of the community—pass by the wounded man without stopping. Surely members of Jesus' audience would have considered these two to be the man's neighbors, yet neither of them tries to help. Next a Samaritan comes down the road. This man would not have brought the word *neighbor* to mind for Jesus' audience. In fact, they would have regarded him with suspicion as an outsider to the Jewish community. Yet the Samaritan is the one who bandages the injured man's wounds, picks him up, puts him on his own pack animal, takes him to an inn, and cares for him there.

The lesson, of course, is that our neighbor is not necessarily the one who looks like us. Our neighbor may not belong to our community. Our neighbor may be the person we have avoided or even despised, yet he or she may be the very one we will need for our survival. The crime against the traveling man in Jesus' story evokes a crisis. In that crisis, he discovers that he needs others; he needs the compassion of the total stranger who is, in fact, his neighbor.

Large or small, setbacks can remind us of our need for others. When we encounter a setback and seek help, we discover neighbors everywhere. Even those we once regarded with suspicion have something to offer us, but it takes the reversal to teach us this lesson. The gift of the setback, therefore, is a deeper awareness of and reliance upon the fabric of human interrelatedness. If everyone, even the casual passerby, is a neighbor upon whom we may depend, then we are never truly alone. By asking for and receiving help in a time of setback, we learn that help is available when we need it, and this fact sends us out into the world with greater confidence. We are never really alone; help is always close, simply because we are all part of the human family.

Those of us who have experienced emotional wounding may have trouble trusting; we assume that the hurtful experiences will repeat themselves through closeness to another human being. Therapists sometimes use the device of the "crisis card" to remind clients to reach out to trustworthy others. The card lists people to call in a crisis. It serves as a physical reminder of our essential condition of interdependence, openly acknowledging that we need help and that help is available.

Crises and setbacks can teach us the skill of being and having neighbors. They show us, in living color, the fundamental

> Setbacks are
> friends to faith.

relationship of neighbor that Jesus wants us to understand. Loving others as neighbors means that we don't leave one another alone in times of setback and struggle but instead extend ourselves in weakness or strength—we connect by offering and receiving help.

DEPENDENCE ON GOD

Setbacks are friends to faith. The difficulties we have in maintaining our discipline remind us—or teach us—that even in our efforts to do good, we need God. Fallible and human, we easily forget this fact when things are going well. On the other hand, when we make mistakes, we remember our humanity and faith. We are merely human, and God is God.

Dependence on God forms the foundation of true humility, and our experience of dependence—so easily forgotten—returns to us in our weaker moments. When I try to pray and my mind wanders, even this tiny setback can remind me of my humanity, my vulnerability, and my need for God. Larger setbacks give us even stronger lessons about who we are. In his book *Let Your Life Speak*, Parker J. Palmer describes a lesson he received about humility through a depressive episode: "Depression was, indeed, the hand of a friend trying to press me down to ground on which it was safe to stand —the ground of my own truth, my own nature, with its complex mix of limits and gifts, liabilities and assets, darkness and light."[6] Palmer's depression taught him that he had overstretched himself; he had tried to do work that was not truly his to do, work that did not match his natural inclinations and gifts. His failures in the work, accompanied by depression, felt like setbacks; yet they were actually friends, drawing him back to himself so that he could experience life with authenticity and joy.

Setbacks can cultivate true humility, the capacity to be one's true self. They remind us of our glorious calling to be ourselves before God and the world—not greater or less than any other human being, yet always subject to and reverent toward God, who exceeds all that we are.

I have often overstretched my own human limitations, even with the best of intentions, trying to do the world some good. While in divinity school, I idolized my priest, a young, down-to-earth, inspiring activist. She had founded and managed a nonprofit program to help women make the transition from jail back into society. She gave weekly sermons that made people laugh and cry. She was passionate and creative, a natural leader. And I wanted to be just like her—what could be more noble? I aspired to do good in the world, to do the kind of good she did, and this seemed to me a worthwhile pursuit.

Unfortunately, in my efforts to be just like my priest, I encountered one setback after another. I reached my limit when I tried to begin a nonprofit program like the one she had started. Only a week into planning the program, I realized that I had no passion for the work. The program was a great idea, but that alone did not suffice; the project did not speak to me. I backed out and felt terrible; this seemed like a setback, a failure. Why couldn't I do this good work?

My father, witnessing my feelings of failure, pointed out that I had not failed but had chosen to be true to myself. This choice honored God's purpose and helped me listen to my calling. He told me, "You are not called to be your priest. You are called to be *you*."

The call to be you lies hidden in many setbacks. Being you means acknowledging your dependence on God in all things, even in doing good work in the world. We need God's help even to serve God. We need to stand on the ground of our own true identities and on God as theologian Paul Tillich's "ground of being." Our very being grows out of God; we do nothing apart from God, and our best work will never be ours alone. When we try to work alone, a blessed setback comes along to remind us to look again for the real place from which our work flows. We return to the God-ground beneath our feet; only then can we do good work and engage in a fruitful discipline.

SELF-FORGIVENESS

Yet another lesson embedded in setback is self-forgiveness—the art of being gentle with ourselves, treating ourselves as we would anyone else who has made a mistake. Scripture does not teach self-forgiveness, but we find its foundation there. The Bible enjoins us to forgive repeatedly—Peter asked, "How often should I forgive? As many as seven times?" Jesus said to him, "Not seven times, but, I tell you, seventy-seven times" (Matt. 18:21-22). Since the Bible exhorts us to forgive our neighbors so consistently and generously and to love our neighbors as ourselves, then it seems we ought to treat ourselves and our neighbors equally, even in matters of forgiveness. Jesus implies that we need to love ourselves, to extend ourselves the same kindness and compassion we show our neighbors.

At times we can more easily forgive our neighbors than ourselves. Many of us are trained to treat others gently but hold ourselves to high standards. Also, seeing ourselves objectively is challenging, locked as we are in our own minds. To forgive ourselves, we have to see ourselves as we would see another person. When another person hurts me, I am aware of hurt coming from outside myself. I know where the hurt originated. I can identify the wrong committed and can then choose to forgive it. But when hurt comes from inside myself—through some form of self-criticism or self-blame—understanding what happened is harder. I may have a vague feeling of guilt; but unless I stop to think, I may not know where the feeling came from. I must consciously monitor the ways I hurt myself, and from there I can begin to understand and forgive my own actions.

Setbacks give us ample opportunity to practice self-forgiveness. Every time we slip up in some new habit or discipline, we have an opportunity. We come to a crossroads: we can choose to say judgmental statements to ourselves, or we can say gentle, forgiving statements. The most difficult part comes in noticing the crossroads. Once we notice the choice before us between judgment and forgiveness, we can choose to forgive. Many of us err on the side of self-criticism, thinking that this will reinforce our commitment to discipline. The habit of self-forgiveness, however, makes us no less faithful to our committed discipline; it simply acknowledges that we will slip up because we are human. And like all human beings, we deserve forgiveness for our slips.

Self-forgiveness does not mean pretending that nothing happened or removing ourselves from all accountability. Rather, it means acknowledging what happened without judging. To forgive ourselves, we speak the truth in love, saying to ourselves, "You did that, and I forgive you for it." This forgiveness allows us to let go of the incident and move forward.

Any change we undertake will involve setbacks. Learning the art of self-forgiveness benefits not only us but also those around us. As we practice forgiving ourselves, we improve our capacity for all sorts of forgiveness, and our forgiveness spills out into the world many times over. With each act of forgiveness we increase our overall capacity for compassion and love, and in doing so become better imitators of Christ.

REFLECTION QUESTIONS

1. When has your Lenten practice faltered? How did you feel when that happened?

2. When you have slipped in your practice or made another mistake, what enabled you return to the practice?

3. How have setbacks renewed your commitment to a discipline? How have they made you more aware of your need for others and your dependence on God?

4. When have you been able to forgive yourself for making a mistake? What made this self-forgiveness possible?

5. Read Psalm 16 and imagine yourself protected and rescued by God as the psalmist describes. How might such rescue restore your energy after a setback? How are you shown "the path of life" (v. 11)?

Week 6

consecration

Remove the sandals from your feet, for the place on
which you are standing is holy ground.

—Exodus 3:5

If you imagine a land cleared and cultivated, prepared and
blessed with new growth, Holy Week is the time of its consecration. This week, we watch for ways in which God blesses
the work we have done, filling it with the holy and dedicating
its coming fruits to the upbuilding of the kingdom.

As a time of consecration, this week is a time to think of
our cleared ground as holy. Moses' experience on the mountain
of God teaches us about holy ground. On one ordinary workday, Moses chooses to lead his flock of sheep beyond the
wilderness to Horeb, the mountain of God. There he encounters a bush that burns but is not consumed by the flames.
Drawn to this bizarre sight, he stares at it. Then a voice emanating from the bush calls his name: "Moses, Moses!" Moses
responds, "Here I am." The voice warns, "Come no closer!
Remove the sandals from your feet, for the place on which you
are standing is holy ground." The voice identifies itself to
Moses: "I am the God of your father, the God of Abraham, the

God of Isaac, and the God of Jacob." Moses, realizing the enormity of the presence before him, hides his face (Exod. 3:1-6).

In our cleared space during this week, we behave differently, as Moses does on Horeb. At first Moses seems to blunder in, walking around as he would anywhere. But when he discovers the place's significance, he acts quite differently: he stops moving, takes off his shoes, hides his face. By removing his shoes, he places himself in God's presence with vulnerability and self-revelation. He exposes the tender soles of his feet directly to the holy ground. By hiding his face, he deprives himself of the sense we most often use to take in information about the world. He stops looking at God with his eyes, which we use to make quick assessments, and he relates to God by stepping beyond his ordinary senses, by seeing God with an inner eye.

This week we will engage in a series of meditations on the holy. Like Moses, we approach God's holy ground with our shoes removed and our eyes closed: vulnerable, open, trusting, trying hard to see our way toward the holy of holies using an inner eye. This land we stand on, land we have worked ourselves, is converted into a strange place, one utterly transformed by God's presence, and we can explore it with an inner sense, trusting God to guide us closer to Godself.

LAST SUPPER: HOLY SELF-GIVING

In the Passover meal we have come to call the Last Supper, Jesus chooses to share himself—his very body and blood—with his dearest friends. Christ gives not only bread and wine to his disciples present in that moment, but he also gives them a ritual of remembrance. The thought of leaving his friends, men to whom he felt close and with whom he had formed a community, must have grieved him. It makes sense that he wanted to give them a way to remember him so they would not feel so alone without him. His intimate, self-giving gesture

INDIVIDUAL EXERCISE

Near the beginning of Holy Week, create a sacred space in your home. You might use an entire room or just a corner or alcove. Design the space so it feels comfortable and welcoming, including furniture or pillows to sit on. Bring into the space any objects you regard as sacred—books, photos, candles, nature objects, icons, or other sacred symbols. Display them in such a way that you feel surrounded by them.

Enter this space each day this week and allow yourself to rest in it. As you relax, imagine yourself and the space filled with holiness. Pray, using words if you like, or pray without words by sitting quietly in God's presence.

meant they had something to hold on to, something they could touch and taste, something to keep Christ close. In the Last Supper, Jesus gives the gift of himself not only in that moment but for all generations to come, promising his intimate presence to all who reenact this supper.

We can mimic Christ's gift by giving of ourselves. The farther we progress in spiritual growth and awareness, the more we become able and willing to give. The Last Supper teaches us the sacredness of our own increasing capacity to give. Often we undertake Christian service because we know we *should*. Everyone at church works in the soup kitchen, and we know it's the right thing to do; it's what Jesus would want us to do. We volunteer out of a sense of obligation, or even—if we look closely and honestly enough—because of peer pressure. As our inner clearing work continues, however, we find a genuine desire to give welling up from a deep place. We find that we actually want to give of ourselves, our time, and our energy, not because we "should" or because we feel guilty but because our hearts have begun to overflow a bit, and they feel lighter when we give away some care. Holy Week consecrates this newfound capacity for self-giving. Having done our clearing work, we now have more self from which to give. We give from a richer place, one flowing with God.

If you can engage in one more practice this week, let it be the practice of finding your new riches—in the place where you have cleared some space—and consider how you feel inspired to give. Your gift may be as simple as listening when a friend needs to talk, or it may be something larger, a commitment to help a community you care about. But be sure your gift comes from a rich, genuine place, the place where you feel God's strength in you, the place that feels truly loving—where you really feel the joy of giving, as Christ must have felt giving himself to his friends.

GARDEN OF GETHSEMANE: HOLY FEAR

Jesus spends the hours before he is taken into custody praying in Gethsemane. In his prayer he asks first that God "remove this cup from me," that he not be required to endure the agony he knows is coming. Luke 22:4 tells us that his sweat was "like great drops of blood falling down on the ground." In his humanness, Jesus must be terrified, and his terror could be considered a form of holy fear. His fear, engendered as it is by his dedication to God's plan, remains consecrated to the plan's unfolding.

Fearful as he may be, Jesus also has the courage to distinguish his will from God's and to ask that God's will be done, not his own. He concludes his prayer with a phrase much like the one we pray so regularly in the Lord's Prayer: "Not my will but yours be done" (Luke 22:42).

Thy will be done. In relation to our ordinary, workaday lives, these may be the most revolutionary words we will ever say. Saying them can change our orientation to life: we put our little boats into a great stream and drop our oars. The prospect of relinquishing our lives to God's will can be terrifying, as it may have been at first for Jesus on that night of prayer in the garden. But this fear comprises part of a holy moment; it is endured and transcended so that God's will may be done.

The work of clearing space is therefore the work of letting go, of saying "Thy will be done." When space is cleared, we lose a bit of our old control over things; we clear the space and allow God to fill it, agreeing to tend whatever growth God engenders. The experience can be scary. We may wonder what will come up and miss our old ways of doing things and our old methods of control. This situation resembles the difference between tending native wildflowers and planting flowers of our own choosing. When we let go, we agree to tend God's wildflower growth; we agree to take a secondary role in our life's project, allowing ourselves to become servants of our growth rather than its masters.

The Hebrew Bible demonstrates this form of letting go through the story of Abraham's willingness to sacrifice Isaac. This story has a disturbing quality. What kind of a father would agree to kill his own son? It seems barbaric, so contrary to all human goodness, and it is hard to imagine that God would ask a man to do this. But this story is not a lesson in how to treat a son; rather, it is a lesson in ultimate trust. It teaches us to put God's will before all else, even above our most powerful instincts and deepest loves, even above love like that of an aging father for his son. Abraham's willingness to let go of his greatest earthly joy demonstrated the extent of his submission to God's will.

We transcend fear by letting go, by saying, "Thy will be done" and trusting that God's will is good. Once we learn to trust that enacting God's will leads to greater human flourishing, fear subsides, and we can move past it.

Clearing space, with its new practices and unfamiliar habits, can leave us feeling exposed or confused, as if we were in a wide-open space with no sure direction. We stand in this open, holy space, waiting to see what will happen, trusting in God's goodness, and possibly sweating as Christ did. We know as he did that suffering may lie ahead. It takes courage and faith in God's purpose to continue our work, to devote ourselves honestly to God's guidance, and to remember the promise: we will find our lives by first losing them.

CRUCIFIXION: HOLY SACRIFICE

The Crucifixion is the critical turning point in Holy Week. It is Jesus' pivotal moment of self-surrendering love, the ultimate in letting go—Jesus relinquishes his physical existence, the only life that human beings know, to do God's will and save humankind. At the time of the Crucifixion, before the Resurrection, Jesus' death must have seemed to onlookers like a negation of all he had been and worked for. From their perspective, Jesus had lost his life; before the Resurrection, his sacrifice had no clear meaning. In the Crucifixion, Jesus endures a staggering experience of loss. And this event crystallizes Lent in a moment; the Crucifixion shows us the essence of what we are doing, if we allow ourselves to experience it closely. The Crucifixion portrays Lent's painful loss of worldly self and the faith that God's purpose makes this loss necessary and meaningful.

All of Lent is a lesson in giving up pieces of ourselves. Meister Eckhart, a fourteenth-century Christian mystic, said that the spiritual life is not so much a process of addition as a process of subtraction. In other words, the closer we wish to come to God, the more of our carefully constructed selves we must relinquish. We have to give up our illusions, our defenses, any selfish personal goals, our carefully designed sense of who we are supposed to be and what we are supposed to do. This sounds terrible, and it can be painful. However, as we give up these areas, we open our-

> All of Lent is a lesson in giving up pieces of ourselves.

selves, and God enters more fully. Into the new space, created by the process of subtraction, comes God's reality, God's hopes and dreams for humankind, God's sense of who we are supposed to be and what we are supposed to do. The hard part—the part involving faith—is to trust in the goodness of this process, because it can feel like one giant loss after another.

We endure Lent's process of subtraction because it opens us wider; the process of subtraction brings us closer to God, where true life is to be found. This is the true purpose behind any small sacrifices we have made this season. We muster all the faith that we can and lose what we feel called to lose, trusting beyond reason, beyond our senses, that God is working powerfully in and through us.

Mother Teresa heard God's voice telling her to go to India to serve the poor and the sick. She thought this task sounded absolutely awful, and she had no desire to go. But the voice she heard was so indisputably God's and its sweetness so complete and enticing that she couldn't say no. Eventually she stopped hearing God's voice, yet she stayed in India and devoted her life to serving God by ministering to human beings in need. Every day of Mother Teresa's work must have been an act of holy sacrifice—a crucifixion of sorts—in which she chose not to live for herself but for God.[7]

Every day of Lent, we have cleared away things to make room for God. Believe that this self-sacrifice has been and remains holy, and trust that God will fill your empty spaces with unimagined abundance. Step off into the abyss, trusting that you will be caught as Jesus was, that your sacrifice will be used for the good of the world.

HOLY SATURDAY: HOLY SHADOW

According to the Apostles' Creed, Jesus descended into hell in the interim between his crucifixion and resurrection. Christ's descent into hell illustrates the wideness of God's mercy: in fact, the Crucifixion saves not only the living but also the dead. Christ's salvation is universal, reaching even into the very depths of hell. Christ descended into hell to shed his light throughout the world, to good and evil, living and dead. This doctrine affects us personally; if we are serious in our efforts to become more Christlike, we must also be ready to allow light into the deepest, darkest place we can imagine—even into the dark places in ourselves.

Carl Jung, the noted psychoanalyst, believed that each person had a shadow side; all the qualities that a person has but has disowned comprise this shadow. For example, a woman might view herself as sweet, having been told from childhood what a sweet person she is. "Sweet" becomes her primary identity, and any thought or action that does not fit with "sweet" becomes part of her shadow. She suppresses anger, frustration, and critical tendencies because they do not fit with her "sweet" image. Unexpressed, her shadow self gains power and fury, trying to get out, trying to achieve expression.

This Holy Saturday, marked by Jesus' descent into hell, could be our opportunity to reach out to our shadow side, the parts of ourselves that we know exist but shroud in darkness. Just as Jesus carried his love into hell, so we can give love to the disowned parts of ourselves. We can consecrate the shadow side on this Holy Saturday, giving it compassion and redeeming it by incorporating it into our being.

Our efforts to clear space in our lives may have revealed bits of our shadow self. On Holy Saturday, no matter how distasteful those aspects may be, remember that they are made holy by Christ's presence. I find that I can only accept disowned aspects of myself in small increments. For instance, when I engage in my own practice of meditation and prayer, I come face-to-face with my own fears. If I don't bother to make space for prayer in my life, I can live in relative ease, pretending that my fears don't exist and finding various crafty ways of hiding them from myself.

When I clear space in my life, I see my fears face-to-face. My fearful shadow self emerges, and I have to admit my vulnerability and weakness. To redeem this part of my shadow, I can allow Christ's presence to enter it. Christ's presence with my shadow shows me that fear does serve a purpose. A little fear keeps us safe; it keeps us from walking off cliffs or putting our hands in fires. Human beings don't want to get rid of fear entirely. When I realize the value of my fear, I can let my fear serve its true purpose in my life. I can allow fear to protect me, when appropriate, and I can thank it for its efforts and set it aside when I don't need it. When my fear is thus redeemed, it subsides; the fear comes out of the shadow and becomes part of the self that lives in the light.

This Holy Saturday might be considered the day of the holy shadow, the day your disowned parts become consecrated. They are holy; they make up who you are as a child of God. No matter how distasteful, no matter how much you might consign your disowned parts to the shadows, Christ is there to redeem them, to incorporate them, to draw them into the light of salvation.

EASTER VIGIL

Holy Week's final consecration is that of the holy vigil, the time of keeping watch. In these hours, we sit and wait, trying to stay alert. A vigil is a lonely time, like the hours spent awake after others have gone to sleep. We tend to think of

Easter Vigil as a weighty obligation, a time to sit and ponder Christ's sacrifice for us. Such pondering certainly has a place, but in its essence, a vigil is simply a period of alert, dedicated presence. As we await Easter morning, the vigil is our way of saying to Christ, "We are with you. We are paying attention." Vigil is a holy, intimate time that we spend with Christ, a time that makes our clearing work possible. We have cultivated a capacity for open alertness through our Lenten practice, and now we have an opportunity to use it. The Easter Vigil offers a chance to watch for signs of divinity all around us, and it is an act of homage to the One who redeems us.

A conscious walk in the woods is a good practice for learning to keep vigil. Unlike an ordinary hike in which you might talk to a friend or puzzle over life's problems, the vigil-walk is one in which you think as little as possible. Instead, you clear your mind and let the natural world appear to you without gloss or interpretation, just as it is.

In her essay "Living Like Weasels," Annie Dillard wonders how a weasel thinks, and she concludes that its attention is focused entirely on the present moment, riveted to reality by physical senses and the necessities of life in the wild.[8] Such focus on the present is the kind of attention vigil calls for. Much like Christ's reminder that today's worries will suffice for today, the practice of vigil teaches us to focus on the present.

The practice of the vigil-walk is as follows:

1. Clear your mind. Recognize outside thoughts as they come, and let them move through your mind without giving them excessive attention or struggle. Plan to return to them when the walk is over.

2. Begin walking. Attend to the world around you—grasses, trees, birds; or if you are in a city, notice buildings, people, cars. Notice not only sights but smells and sounds. Take it all in, and, as much as you can, do

nothing with the information. Don't interpret anything or analyze what you see and hear. Just perceive; use your senses and sense. For the duration of this vigil-walk, nothing exists except this moment; you are alert, expecting anything, open to anything.

This practice provides a small example of what Buddhists and Christians call *mindfulness,* and it forms the essence of vigil. Vigil is attentive openness, and with our clearing work done, we have cultivated just the kind of openness we need to do vigil well. At this time, in the final hours of Lent, we consecrate our openness, our vigil, to Christ and await the full flower of Easter morning.

REFLECTION QUESTIONS

1. How have you encountered the holy this week? When have you felt awestruck or humbled?

2. How does God sanctify your self-giving and sacrifice? How does God reach out to bless your fear and your shadow?

3. Have you had an opportunity to keep vigil this week? What did you observe through your open watchfulness?

4. Read about Jesus' prayer on the Mount of Olives in Luke 22:39-44. Imagine him there, imagine his surroundings, and imagine the holiness with which he imbues the place. What prayers do you wish to offer in this holy place?

epilogue:
easter sunday

No matter how small you feel your change during this season has been, no matter how personal and limited, it affects the world. Because we are relational beings, constantly engaged with our environments, our orientation toward the world affects the world for good or ill. Even our inner work changes the world, because it changes our orientation; it alters the messages we send out and our response to messages received. As we have done our own personal clearing work, we have allowed more of God's love to flow through us, like light through clear water, into the world. By creating this sort of transparency, even on such a small and personal scale, we contribute more to the kingdom than we can comprehend. A soul in deeper communion with God draws the entire world a little closer to God.

On Easter morning, we celebrate Christ's resurrection, which is more than just a return to life; it is a new, stronger, never-ending life. At the same time, we emerge from Lent as new people, transformed by our time in the wilderness and by the work we did there. We partake of Christ's eternal life because we have chosen to make room for it in ourselves. We begin to live not merely as physical beings but to tap into the spiritual source of our life. This transformation, from old to new, from chaotic to cleared, culminates in the inbreaking of light on Easter morning.

As you celebrate this Easter, think back to your experience of the wilderness early in Lent. Remember how you cleared space—gradually, sometimes painfully, and other times joyfully. Now enjoy the freedom you feel in your clearing. Celebrate its ongoing transformation into a garden, and know that God guards and tends this garden with you today and every day from now on.

group exercises

GROUP SIZE

The ideal group size for the following Lenten exercises is from six to eight people. Keeping the group small allows plenty of time for each group member to talk. However, some group members may drop out before the season is over, so an initial group of eight to ten people may be appropriate. A larger group could also work, provided that members understand that individual participation time will be limited.

MATERIALS NEEDED

- Candle; matches or lighter
- Pens and paper
- Chalkboard or marker board; if neither is available, bring a flip chart.

FIRST SUNDAY IN LENT: ORGANIZATIONAL MEETING

Preparation: Arrive a few minutes early, if possible. Arrange chairs in a circle, and place the candle in a visible spot. Set up the flip chart if the room has no chalkboard or marker board. Sit for a few minutes in silence, allowing yourself to picture God's presence filling the room and blessing the upcoming meeting.

Opening: After all the group has arrived, light the candle and ask someone to read aloud Psalm 51:10-12. If group members do not already know you or one another, have all introduce themselves, giving their names and reasons for joining the group.

Introduce the notion of clearing space during Lent, encouraging members to view the next six weeks as God's invitation to a fuller life. Ask group members to consider areas of their lives that feel cluttered or blocked and to imagine how clearing space might allow them more contact with God.

Explain that the group will engage in weekly activities, and ask members to read each chapter *before* the group meeting that pertains to the chapter. For example, they will read Week 1, "Exploring the Wilderness," before the next group meeting. Also tell them they can read the book in small sections. Because the first section of each chapter contains an individual activity for the week, readers will benefit from reading at least that section early in the week.

Outline the dates and times of all future group meetings so members know what to expect. Also, in this first meeting you may wish to establish ground rules for the group. Ground rules create a sense of safety among members, allowing them to open up to one another more readily and derive greater benefits from the group experience. The members can agree upon ground rules together. You may want to suggest the following ground rules as a starting point:

- We will maintain confidentiality. We will not repeat anything heard in the group outside our group meetings.

- We will ask a group member's permission before commenting on his or her statements, thoughts, actions, and so forth. (This rule's purpose is to encourage open sharing, nonjudgmental listening, and respect for one another's experiences. Members will feel safer sharing if they can do so without fear of negative feedback from other members.)

The group may create its own rules in addition to these. Write the ground rules on the board or flip chart.

Reflections: Invite group members to discuss their feelings about Lent. Ask: "What are your preconceptions about Lent? Have you given up something for Lent in the past? If so, describe your experience." Allow members to express any concerns or hopes they have about the coming six weeks.

Activity: Distribute pens and paper, and ask group members to write down one sentence expressing their greatest hope related to participating in the group and working through the season. Tell them that no one will see what they write; they will take the piece of paper home with them and keep it until the end of the season. Allow a few minutes of silence for members to think and write. When they finish, offer a prayer of consecration over the slips of paper and the hopes written on them.

Closing: Offer the following prayer.

> O Lord, who sends us into the wilderness and protects us there, bless our time together this Lent. Help us to guide and support one another on this journey. Make our work yours, so that everything we do this season opens us safely to ourselves, to one another, and to you. Amen.

> *Leader:* Go in peace to love and serve the Lord.
> *Group:* Thanks be to God.

SECOND SUNDAY IN LENT:
EXPLORING THE WILDERNESS

Preparation: Arrive a few minutes early to arrange the chairs, set up the candle, and center yourself before the group members arrive.

Opening: When all have gathered, have one person light the candle as another reads aloud Mark 1:12-13.

Reflections: Ask group members to recall their own experiences of wilderness in the previous week. Offer pens and paper and ask members to write about or draw their experience, using whatever images emerged when they engaged in silent meditation during the previous week. If they did not do the meditation, describe the wilderness elements: being driven out of one's comfort zone, encountering temptations, wild beasts, and angels. Ask them to reflect silently on their own wilderness and to render the images that appear to them using words or drawings. Allow a few minutes for the group members to work on this activity.

When everyone has finished, invite group members to share their writings and drawings if they wish. Do not force anyone who prefers not to share, but allow time for everyone who wishes to speak. Encourage group members to talk about both the positive and negative aspects of their experience of wilderness and to share any insights gained from the experience.

Activity: When everyone who wishes to has spoken, invite the group members to sit comfortably and relax. To create a peaceful atmosphere in the room, turn off the lights or play soft background music. As the group members relax, ask them to picture the wilderness they experienced in the previous week. Ask them to imagine it vividly. Say, "Picture yourself walking from this room into the wilderness you discovered last week. See the vegetation and the terrain change around you as they transform into ever-deeper wilderness. Imagine wildlife around you; see how the place is overgrown and untended. As you arrive in the deepest part of the wilderness, look around and observe. What are the trees and grasses like? What animals live here? What is the light like? How do you feel in this place? Imagine yourself standing still in this wilderness." *(Allow a moment of silence.)* "After you have stood still for a moment, imagine God entering the wilderness to be with you. Picture God in any form that has meaning for you—as a light, as a sense of warmth, or in the person of Christ. Allow yourself to be enveloped in God's loving presence. As you rest in God, imagine the space around you changing, becoming filled with God's presence. What happens now to the trees and grasses, the animals, the light in this place? How does the wilderness look as it is transformed by God? When the space around you is clear enough that you begin to feel comfortable and at ease, leave the spot where you have been standing and begin to make your way back. Know that you can return to the wilderness whenever you like. Imagine yourself walking slowly back to this room, letting God continue to bless the space you leave behind for now."

Invite group members to talk about the guided meditation, sharing any feelings that arose and talking about what space they envisioned, both in its original and transformed states.

Closing: Remind group members that they will choose a Lenten practice in the coming week. Encourage them to choose a practice that clears some space in the wilderness they have imagined. Remind them also to consider their hopes for the season (that they wrote on slips of paper last week) as they choose a practice. Ask the group members to choose a practice they can do regularly and one that is reasonable—not too big to accomplish over the coming six weeks. If they have trouble thinking of practices, direct them to the appendix or encourage them to ask other group members for help.

Offer a closing prayer, giving thanks for the work of the previous week and blessing the week to come. Conclude by saying:

Leader: Go in peace to love and serve the Lord.
Group: Thanks be to God.

Third Sunday in Lent: First Clearing

Preparation: Prepare, as for the other sessions, by arranging chairs in a circle. For this session, you will need pens or pencils and paper for the group members. Markers or crayons will help, as some members may wish to draw.

Opening: Ask one person to light the candle as another reads aloud Joel 2:12-13.

Reflections: Invite group members to describe their experiences in the previous week. Individuals may wish to share their insights into their own defenses, and if they tried stepping outside their defenses, they may wish to describe that experience. Ask the group, "What vulnerability did you express to God this week?" Some members may not feel comfortable answering this question publicly, which is fine. They may, however, be able to talk about how it felt to be vulnerable—was it frightening, liberating, some combination of those two feelings?

Activity: Ask group members to consider silently their experience of beginning Lenten practices during the previous week. Invite them to reflect more deeply on the vulnerability or emotion that this practice calls for. They may recall feelings of fear, reluctance, grief, confusion, or ones of excitement, hopefulness, or peace. Ask the group members to maintain silence for a moment and to touch the place in their own hearts that the new practices open up.

After the silence, ask the group members to draw their "broken" hearts—the soft inner core opened up by their Lenten practices. Let them know that they can use colors, representational images, or abstract design. There is no right way to draw the inner heart; the drawing simply represents vulnerability and emotion meaningfully for the individual.

When the group finishes, invite people to share their drawings with the group as they feel comfortable. After those who wish have talked about their drawings, instruct the group members to take the drawings home and put them in a place that feels safe and sacred to them. In doing so they symbolically place their vulnerable hearts in God's care.

Closing: With each member holding the writing, drawing, or other symbol he or she created, offer the following prayer of blessing:

> Loving God, we thank you for the protection that our hardened hearts have offered in the past. We ask now that you offer us a dynamic, living protection as we move beyond some of our defenses and open our hearts to you and to others. Bless and care for the tender, hidden contents of our hearts. We ask that your light may shine in our darkness and that the darkness will not overcome it. Amen.

Leader: Go in peace to love and serve the Lord.
Group: Thanks be to God.

FOURTH SUNDAY IN LENT: NATURAL RHYTHMS

Preparation: Arrive a few minutes early and arrange the chairs in a circle. Spend a few minutes reading Ecclesiastes 3:1-8 quietly and reflecting on the passage. Again imagine God's presence filling the room in preparation for the group members' arrival.

Opening: Have one person light the candle, and ask another to read aloud Psalm 19:1-4.

Reflections: Invite members to describe their experiences of the previous week. Ask the group to consider the following questions, presenting the questions one at a time: "What rhythms did you observe in your practice? How did you discern between rhythms that felt natural and ones that felt imposed? Did you at any time have to force yourself to engage in the practice?"

Activity: When the group has finished talking about the previous week, transition into the next part of the session by asking group members to close their eyes. Invite them to relax and listen carefully as you read aloud Ecclesiastes 3:1-8. After the reading, talk about the rhythms described in the passage: "This passage mentions that there is a time for everything, and there is also a time for its opposite. We move back and forth between different appropriate activities at different times in our lives."

Now ask the participants to hear the passage again, this time listening for any particular phrases that speak to them. Ask them to notice which words jump to their attention. Invite them to close their eyes as you read the passage a second time.

After the second reading, ask group members to pair up and discuss with their partner the parts of the passage that spoke to them. Ask them to consider the following questions together: "Why did that phrase speak to you? If you identified with one activity in the passage (for instance, "a time to plant"), how did you feel about its opposite ("a time to pluck up what is planted")? How have you moved back and forth between the two activities described in the phrase that spoke to you?"

Return to the full group after five minutes of discussion in pairs. Invite individuals to share their insights with the full group if they wish.

Closing: Remind the group that developing a meaningful spiritual practice takes time, and encourage them to continue experimenting with different rhythms for their practice until they find one that feels right. Offer the following closing prayer:

> Loving God, help us find the rhythms that are as natural to us as the rhythms of day and night. Bless our efforts and let them bring us ever closer to you. Help us so attune ourselves to your rhythms that we do nothing apart from you. Amen.

Leader: Go in peace to love and serve the Lord.
Group: Thanks be to God.

FIFTH SUNDAY IN LENT: NEW GROWTH

Preparation: If you have a small plant you can bring to this session, bring it and place it next to the candle to symbolize the new growth taking place in group members this week. As usual, arrange the chairs in a circle and take time to center yourself and invite God's presence with the group.

Opening: Have one member light the candle, and ask another to read aloud Ephesians 3:14-21.

Reflections: Ask group members to share the ways in which they have experienced new growth as a result of their Lenten practice. Remind them of evidences of new growth: increased creativity, capacity for love, and openness to surprise. If any individuals have difficulty finding evidence of new growth, ask other group members for help; if a member describes his or her practice to the group, the group may see growth in it that the member cannot see.

Activity: Remind the group of the Ephesians verse, read at the beginning of the session, that speaks of being "rooted and grounded in love." Ask group members to imagine the new growth they have discovered this season being rooted and grounded in love—to imagine their growth springing from the ground of God's love as it lives in them. Group members may visualize the growth in their lives as an actual plant, emerging from the ground of love. Distribute pens (or crayons) and paper, and ask group members to describe or draw their new growth, using words, images, or some combination of the two.

When everyone finishes, allow group members to share their descriptions and images with one another. Ask them to tell why they chose particular words or images.

Closing: Read Ephesians 3:14-21 again, offering it as a prayer of gratitude for and blessing upon the new growth that is emerging.

Leader: Go in peace to love and serve the Lord.
Group: Thanks be to God.

SIXTH SUNDAY IN LENT (PASSION/PALM SUNDAY): WEATHERING STORMS

Preparation: Before this session, take time to consider any setbacks you have experienced and to think about not only the pain they caused but also the benefits you derived from them. After you have arranged the chairs in a circle, take a moment to sit with God in the quiet and give thanks for your own setbacks and for the compassion they inspire in you for others.

Opening: After everyone arrives, have one member light the candle and ask another to read Matthew 18:12-14.

Reflections: Hand out pens and paper. Give the group members a few minutes to consider any setbacks they have experienced, particularly in their Lenten practices. Ask them to identify one they'd like to focus on. With that setback in mind, ask them to think of one or two benefits they gained from it. Remind them of some possible benefits: renewed commitment to the practice, an awareness of their need for others, and a sense of their dependence on God. After they have had time to make a few notes, go around the group, inviting members to share their thoughts. If a group member can name a setback but cannot name any benefits derived from it, invite him or her to ask the group for help. The member may wish to describe the setback and its effects; the other group members can help him or her discern benefits that might not have been apparent at the time. As usual, allow members to "pass" if they prefer not to share.

Activity: Ask group members to close their eyes and relax, and offer the following guided meditation. First, read Matthew 18:12-14 aloud again. Then read the following guided meditation:

Imagine yourself walking down a path in the wilderness you pictured at the beginning of Lent. Visualize your surroundings—see the wilderness looking much as it looked at the beginning of the season. Picture the path you are walking on, and see any trees, brush, or other wildlife surrounding it. Now imagine that you choose to leave the path and walk into uncultivated areas next to the path. Picture yourself moving farther and farther from the path, letting it recede into the distance until you can no longer see it. With the path far behind you, let any feelings you have about leaving the path come into your awareness. Do you feel afraid? confused? uncertain? What do your surroundings look like now? Are they overgrown? Do they seem dangerous?

As you stand there, imagine God coming toward you. You may imagine God in any form that speaks to you—as a light, as a warm presence, or as Christ. Imagine that God finds you standing alone and that God knows how you feel. God acknowledges your feelings and wraps them in kindness and compassion. You find that you are being led gently back toward the path. See the path come into view again, and feel yourself being led gradually toward it. When you meet it, step back onto the path and turn in the direction to which you are guided. Begin moving on the path again, and feel God's continued presence with you as you move. As you begin to move, gradually become aware of yourself in the present moment again.

Closing: Explain that the group needs to choose a sacred place to meet for the Easter session. Discuss spaces that feel sacred to various people, and select a place. (Possibilities include gardens, other natural areas, labyrinths, and sanctuaries.) Plan to meet at the designated place or to travel there together. Offer a closing prayer, giving thanks for setbacks and asking God's guidance in them.

Leader: Go in peace to love and serve the Lord.
Group: Thanks be to God.

EASTER SUNDAY: CONSECRATION

Preparation: If possible, visit the selected sacred space before the session. Look for a convenient gathering spot where people could sit in a circle for the "Reflections" part of the session. On the day of the session, try to arrive early to arrange the space and invite God's presence into it. Remember to bring the candle that the group has been using all season.

Opening: Ask one group member to light the candle while another reads aloud John 20:19-22.

Reflections: Invite the group members, gathered in a circle, to share their experiences of the holy in the previous week. How did this week differ from the previous five weeks? How did individuals experience God's presence more closely this week, and how did they feel in relation to that presence?

Activity: Invite the group to consider the disciples' experience of the resurrected Christ as he entered the space where they were hiding in fear. Read John 20:19-22 again, asking them to imagine themselves in that room, in Christ's holy presence.

Next, invite group members to explore silently the sacred space they have chosen. Ask them to take in as much of it as they can—sights, sounds, and smells. Encourage them to notice the ways in which it feels sacred to them. As they move through the space, ask them to imagine the resurrected Christ present in this space as in the room with the disciples. Ask: "How do you find yourself behaving? How are your senses altered or perceptions heightened? How do you know that this place is sacred?"

Allow plenty of time for this exercise, ten to fifteen minutes, setting a particular amount of time so that everyone knows when to return.

After the set amount of time elapses, bring the group back together to share their experiences of the space. Ask how group members experienced Christ during their silent time.

Closing: Use the following guided meditation.

Imagine yourself walking from this place into your Lenten wilderness. As you walk through it, you arrive at a clearing, the clearing created by your work this season. Notice how this part of the wilderness has changed, how it has become like a garden. See the life that blooms in it; notice how well-tended it is, and see that it looks vibrant and healthy. Feel the sun's warmth in this garden, and observe the ways in which it nurtures the life around you.

Rest here for a moment. Allow yourself, the ground below your feet, and all that grows from it to absorb God's consecration. Notice how love flows into and out of you as you sit in this space. *(Allow a few moments of silence.)* Remain in this holy place as long as you wish, and, when you are ready, return to the present moment.

Offer a prayer of thanksgiving for the group members' time together, express joy at the inbreaking of God's light on Easter morning, and ask God's blessing on the Easter season to come.

Leader: Go in peace to love and serve the Lord. Alleluia, alleluia.

Group: Thanks be to God. Alleluia, alleluia.

appendix:
suggested lenten
practices

At the beginning of Week 2, you will choose a Lenten practice. If you have difficulty choosing one, the following list of suggestions may help.

Daily prayer/meditation time: While this practice seems simple, it can be a profoundly meaningful way to make space for God. For persons beginning the practice of prayer, spending just a few minutes a day at a regular time allows the practice to take root and deepen.

Media fast: A media fast involves abstaining from watching TV, listening to music, or even reading. You might choose to eliminate only certain media, such as television. Or you might restrict your fast to certain hours of the day; for instance, you could choose not to watch TV from 7:00 to 9:00 PM each day. This small change opens space for new activities.

Meditative walks: The practice of a daily, mindful walk can help you feel God's presence more directly. As in the case of prayer, begin by setting aside a small amount of time if this is a new practice. Even a ten-minute walk each day changes one's orientation, especially if you approach this time as a walk with God.

Art: If the arts interest you, consider setting aside some time each day to engage in creative activity. By understanding creativity as a channel for God's creative action in the world, you can view daily time spent creating as time spent with God. You then allow God's energy to move into the world through the work of art.

Journaling: A daily practice of writing can also help you engage with God more deeply. You may be able to set aside just a few minutes each day to write out your thoughts, but as with the other practices, the amount of time spent matters less than the regularity of the practice. Journaling as a spiritual practice may involve simply writing one's thoughts out to God, or it might take a more explicit form of prayers or letters to God.

Community activities: If your spiritual life lacks community involvement, you might choose a Lenten practice of attending church or other community functions throughout the season. At community events, consider how God is made present and how we open ourselves to the possibility that God speaks through others and in human relationships.

Service: Regular service projects are yet another way to come closer to God during Lent. By a practice of regular service, you encounter the presence of Christ in those whom you serve.

notes

1. Ashley Cleveland, "Hope Returned," MethodX.net (Nashville: Upper Room Ministries, 2001), http://www.methodx.net/articles/columns.asp?act=showitem&item_id=63295

2. Shunryu Suzuki, *Zen Mind, Beginner's Mind*, ed. Trudy Dixon (New York: Weatherhill, 1973), 129.

3. Julia Cameron, *The Artist's Way: A Spiritual Path to Higher Creativity* (New York: Penguin Group, 1992).

4. Patricia Skar, "Chaos and Self-Organization: Emergent Patterns at Critical Life Transitions," *Journal of Analytical Psychology* 49 (2004): 243.

5. Erich Fromm, *Psychoanalysis and Religion* (New Haven, Conn.: Yale University Press, 1950), 86.

6. Parker J. Palmer, *Let Your Life Speak: Listening for the Voice of Vocation* (San Francisco: Jossey-Bass, 2000), 67.

7. "Mother Teresa Beatified," *Morning Edition,* NPR, October 14, 2003.

8. Annie Dillard, "Living Like Weasels," in *Teaching a Stone to Talk: Expeditions and Encounters* (New York: Harper & Row, 1988), 11–16.

about the author

SARAH PARSONS works as a psychotherapist with the Pastoral Counseling Centers of Tennessee and at Parthenon Pavilion in Nashville. She holds a BA in Religious Studies from Yale University, a master of divinity from Vanderbilt Divinity School, and a master of social work from the University of Tennessee. Sarah worked at Upper Room Ministries as a Web site editor from 1999 to 2002. She has had articles published in *Weavings, Alive Now, Devo'Zine*, and on MethodX.net.

In her spare time Sarah enjoys running, yoga, other miscellaneous sports, and hanging around in cafés.